Cosmopolitan Democracy

Cosmopolitan Democracy

An Agenda for a New World Order

Edited by
Daniele Archibugi *and* David Held

Polity Press

Copyright © this collection Polity Press, 1995.
Each individual chapter © the author.

First published in 1995 by Polity Press
in association with Blackwell Publishers.

Editorial office:
Polity Press
65 Bridge Street
Cambridge CB2 1UR, UK

Marketing and production:
Blackwell Publishers, the publishing imprint of Basil Blackwell Ltd
108 Cowley Road
Oxford OX4 1JF, UK

Basil Blackwell Inc.
238 Main Street
Cambridge, MA 02142, USA

ISBN 0 7456 1380 2
ISBN 0 7456 1381 0 (pbk)

A CIP catalogue record for this book is available from the British Library
and the Library of Congress.

Typeset in 11 on 13 pt Palatino
by CentraCet Limited, Cambridge
Printed in Great Britain by Hartnolls Ltd,
Bodmin, Cornwall

This book is printed on acid-free paper.

Contents

———

Notes on Contributors

Daniele Archibugi is a researcher at the Italian National Research Council in Rome. He is an adviser to the Organization for Economic Cooperation and Development and to the Commission of the European Union, and has been an Academic Visitor at the Universities of Sussex, Roskilde and Cambridge. He is the coordinator of the European Network on 'The Political Theory of Transnational Democracy'.

Norberto Bobbio is Emeritus Professor of Political Philosophy and Jurisprudence at the University of Turin and a life member of the Italian Senate. His publications include *Democracy and Dictatorship*, *The Future of Democracy* and *The Age of Rights*.

Luigi Bonanate is Professor of International Relations at the University of Turin and Director of Centro di Studi Politici Paolo Farneti. He was President of the Italian Society of Political Science and Vice-President of the University of Turin. His forthcoming book is *Ethics and International Politics*.

Richard Falk is Albert G. Milbank Professor of International Law and Practice at Princeton University. He has been a major contributor to the world order literature for more than three decades. He is one of the original members of the World Order Models Project, which was initiated in 1968, and publishes the journal *Alternatives*. His books include *On Humane Governance, Explorations at the Edge of Time, Revitalizing International Law, Revolutionaries and Functionaries* and *The Promise of World Order*.

David Held is Professor of Politics and Sociology at the Open University. Among his recent publications are *Models of Democracy, Political Theory and the Modern State* and (as editor) *Political Theory Today*. His research interests focus on the changing meaning of democracy in the context of the global economic system and the evolving structures of international decision-making. He is currently completing *The Principle of Autonomy and the Global Order: Foundations of Democracy*.

Mary Kaldor is Reader of International Relations at the European Institute of the University of Sussex. She is cofounder of European Nuclear Disarmament and of the Helsinki Citizens Assembly, and adviser to several international organizations, including the United Nations. Among her books are *The Disintegrating West, The Baroque Arsenal, Europe from Below* and *The Imaginary War: Understanding the East–West Conflict*.

Editors' Introduction

In the space of a few years, we have witnessed sea changes in international relations. For almost half a century, a system of geo-governance organized around the bifurcation of East and West dominated the planet. Almost at a stroke, however, it disintegrated, leaving few clues as to what alternative system might take its place. Now, on the threshold of the third millennium, international politics faces new opportunities and new dangers.

The ending of the confrontation between East and West has dealt a blow (though not yet a death blow) to the most important political phenomenon of the second half of the twentieth century – the possibility of nuclear war. The Cold War international system had a strongly hierarchic structure, with few states able to escape subordination to the overall strategy of the great powers. The division of states into two opposed camps meant that a very limited number of actors was responsible for most of the key political decisions. If, on the one hand, this restricted both participation and democracy, it ensured, on the other, that a certain order was maintained in international affairs. Most states had the job of administering the great strategic decisions taken on the international chessboard in their own territorial squares.

What are we to make of the transformations in international politics of the past few years? These transformations caught most commentators unawares. Up until the last moment, few guessed that the frontiers at the very heart of Europe were about to be redrawn, as they had been on many occasions before 1945. Was not political geography in recent decades an almost carbon-copy of itself, year in, year out? Had not geographical yearbooks virtually disappeared from the shelves of bookshops? Then, territorial boundaries in the East, as well as in the West, were suddenly transformed. The question is: are such transformations indicative of anything more than a temporary shift in power relations as the international community gradually settles into a new hierarchic structure? Or, will such shifts become a distinctive feature of a new phase in history?

The opportunities which offer themselves as the second millennium draws to a close are still waiting to be exploited. If, for a Pole, a Chilean, a Cambodian, a South African or a Palestinian, the ending of the Cold War fosters new hopes for the future, for a Bosnian, a Somali, an Iraqi, a Kurd or a Rwandan the benefits of the 'new world order' are still a long way off. While it is still very early to take stock of the advantages and disadvantages of the end of the Cold War, three crucial questions can be posed to help reflection on the nature of the transition in progress:

1 what are the repercussions on domestic regimes of the new world circumstances?
2 what form of structure will inter-state relations come to crystallize around?
3 which institutions can deliberate and act upon truly global problems?

Each issue should be briefly introduced in order to clarify the themes of the volume as a whole.

(1) Among the domestic political changes of recent years has been the remarkable increase in the number of liberal democratic states. In the East, South and North many states have either been restored to or have newly acquired a democratic system.[1] For the first time in their lives, many millions of people have enjoyed the quintessentially liberal democratic experience of voting in free elections. Although the first steps towards domestic democracy have in many cases been tentative and riddled with contradictions, the first half of the 1990s deserves to be remembered as an, if not the, era of democracy. The desire for democracy has been so strong that some commentators – partly out of optimism, partly out of ignorance of the historical record – have ventured the hypothesis that we are approaching the end of history (cf. David Held's essay in this volume). Yet, despite the geographical extension of liberal democratic regimes, it is also worth emphasizing that for millions of people there has been no noticeable improvement – and in some cases a drastic reduction – in the quality of their political associations.

Paradoxically, while the number of countries governed on the basis of democratic principles has increased, civil war has returned to others in which it was believed to have disappeared for good. The events unfolding in the former Yugoslavia, the former Soviet Union and parts of sub-Saharan Africa show just how traumatic the transition from one regime to another can be. The horrifying civil wars in progress are the tip of the iceberg of unrest to which even the most historically consolidated nation-states are vulnerable. Ethnic conflict and the re-emergence of nationalism in Germany, Italy, Spain, Poland and elsewhere leave little room for an unqualified optimism about the ability of nation-states to keep two of the most important promises on which they were founded – the maintenance of domestic peace and the protection of the safety of their citizens and those citizens' property.

Viewed from the perspective of domestic politics, the emerging world order is two-faced. On the one hand, it has fostered the extension of democracy; on the other hand, it has revealed and, in some cases, detonated the contradictions of nation-states. By imposing a form of limited autonomy on the vast majority of states, the Cold War managed to suppress many forms of domestic conflict – at least in Europe. When the Cold War ended, some of the wounds provoked by domestic discord reopened.

(2) The current historical juncture has not only posed new problems for domestic politics. It has presented, first and foremost, new problems for the organization of inter-state relations. When the old, explicitly established hierarchy of states collapsed, dangerous power voids opened up in the management of international affairs. Democratic countries have reacted to this new situation in a contradictory way. On occasion, they have capitalized on their rival bloc's depleted power by acting unlawfully, as, for instance, the United States did when it intervened in Panama. In other cases, most notably in Kuwait and Iraq, they have sought a consensus of the international community and its institutions before undertaking specific actions.

Generally speaking, however, it is striking that the increase in the number of democratic states has not been accompanied by a corresponding increase in democracy *among* states. Policy-making in institutions like the Security Council and the International Monetary Fund, as well as in more informal settings such as the G7 summits, has changed little since the collapse of the Berlin Wall. National governments, powerful and not so powerful, have continued to act on the basis of their own *reason of state*. The explanation for this has partly to do with an

uncertainty over the appropriate rules, values and institutions necessary to establish greater accountability
among nations. But it has also to do with the reluctance
of democracies to extend their model of governance to
inter-state relations; that is, with their reluctance to be
called to account in matters of security and foreign and
international affairs. It is possible to detect, as Mary
Kaldor does in her essay (Chapter 3), two opposed models
of political organization in Europe – a dominant executive-
led model, and a struggling conception of a more participatory framework for citizens.

(3) The most conspicuous feature of the new international
situation is the emergence of issues which transcend
national frontiers. Processes of economic internationalization, the problem of the environment and the protection
of the rights of minorities are less and less national in
scope and are increasingly a matter for the world community as a whole. The limits on national autonomy
imposed by the balance of terror have now been supplemented by a much subtler, more structural form of
erosion caused by the processes of environmental, social
and economic globalization.

A number of fundamental gaps have opened up
between democratic politics and the late twentieth-
century world, 'gaps' in the relations among citizens,
individual states and the economic system at the regional
and global level. There are at least three 'gaps' worth
noting briefly.[2]

First, there is a gap between the formal domain of
political authority and the actual economic system of
production, distribution and exchange which, with its
many regional and global networks, serves to limit or
undermine the actual power of national political authorities. Second, there is a gap between the idea of the
state as an independent actor and the vast array of

international regimes and organizations which have been established to manage whole areas of transnational activity (trade, the oceans, space, etc). New forms of multinational politics have been established and with them new forms of collective decision-making involving states, intergovernmental organizations and a whole variety of international pressure groups. Third, there is a gap between the idea of membership of a national political community, i.e., citizenship, which bestows upon individuals both rights and duties, and the development of regional and international law which subjects individuals, non-governmental organizations and governments to new systems of regulation. Rights and duties are recognized in international law, moreover, which transcend the claims of nation-states and which, while they may lack coercive powers of enforcement, have far-reaching consequences.

Democratic politics has traditionally presupposed the idea of a 'national community of fate' – a community which rightly governs itself and determines its future. This idea is certainly challenged, if not increasingly undermined, by the nature of the pattern of regional and global interconnections. National communities do not exclusively 'programme the action and decisions of governmental and parliamentary bodies', and the latter by no means simply determine what is right or appropriate for their own citizens.[3]

Of course, there is nothing new about the emergence of global problems. Although their importance has grown considerably, many have existed for decades, if not for much longer. Some were ignored because they were regarded as insoluble due to the rivalry between the great powers. Others have been addressed on the basis of distinctly undemocratic criteria and outside the framework of accountable institutions. Political and strategic decisions, such as those on nuclear weapons, have been taken at USA–USSR summits, while economic issues concerning interest rates and trade balances, for example, have been considered at meetings like that of the G7. The institutions of the United Nations have generally been marginalized; their function has been more one of discussion and representation than of effective management of pressing strategic or socio-economic questions.

Now that the old confrontation between East and West has ended, regional and global problems have returned to the international political agenda. Nonetheless, profound ambiguity still reigns as to which institutions should take supranational decisions and according to what criteria. Superpower summits no longer have the whole world waiting with bated breath, but decisions taken by G7 meetings on economic issues still evade any form of control by public deliberation and opinion, despite the protests of excluded nations and pressures from diverse social groups.

There are, finally, numerous intergovernmental organizations which have proved effective in managing specific issues. For example, postal services, railways, maritime and air traffic are all managed by intergovernmental bodies. All their dealings are publicized, and all states with an interest in the issues in question are involved. Yet, although the standards on which they are based are much more democratic than those underpinning the various summits, they have not been designed for and are not in a position to address more complex problems, such as the environment, the spread of AIDS, the debt crisis of the 'Third World' and economic integration.

Political theory's exploration of emerging global problems is still in its infancy. While democratic theory has examined and debated at length the challenges to democracy that emerge from within the boundaries of the nation-state, it has not seriously questioned whether the nation-state itself can remain at the centre of democratic thought.

The questions posed by the rapid growth of complex interconnections and interrelations between states and societies, along with the evident intersection of national and international forces and processes, remain largely unexplored. And little has been written about the concept and relevance of democracy at the global level. By contrast, the essays in this volume contain reflections and proposals for the construction of a world order imbued with the values of democracy. Although written from a diversity of perspectives, the papers address three central questions: (1) How can the international system contribute to the development of democracy inside states? (2) Is it possible to establish democratic relations among sovereign states? (3) Can decisions which affect the whole world community be taken democratically?

Some dismiss such questions as ill-judged, arguing that everyday political events demonstrate that any form of transnational democracy is an impossible dream. For our part, we believe, despite being aware of the cynical and often brutal methods which characterize many foreign policy decisions, that the extension of democracy to the international sphere is not only desirable but also feasible – in fact, more feasible than at any previous historical moment. However, if it is to have any hope of materialization, what is required, in the first instance, is a new conception of democracy, founded on a new account of international relations and of the possibility of accountability among nations.

Democracy Among Nations

Can some of the central criteria on which national democracy is based be extended to the international community? How can the constitutive principles of democracy such as respect for minorities, the independence of judicial power and the guarantee of fundamental rights also be applied to the international realm? While for a long time political theory has typically regarded democracy as a form of government applicable only inside state boundaries, there have been a few noteworthy exceptions to this rule. One of these is the tradition of 'perpetual peace projects' and subsequently of 'legal pacifism'.[4] For more than three centuries, thinkers within this tradition have sought to create international institutions capable of acting as arbiters between states and, in the final analysis, as the foundation of legally based international relations. The most tangible fruit of these proposals has been the establishment of the League of Nations, the United Nations and other international institutions. Yet, significant though the tradition of legal pacifism has been, it has always lived on the fringe of political theory without ever being integrated into the theory of democracy.

One reason why democratic theorists, no less than international relations theorists, have paid lip service only to the problem of international democracy may lie in the view, at times explicitly stated but often held implicitly, that international democracy can only follow from the achievement of domestic democracy. The argument is that, if all states were to become democratic, the ensuing international regime would be necessarily founded on the principles of democracy.[5] We find a lucid expression of this thesis in Bobbio's essay (Chapter 1). Bobbio summarizes his concerns by posing two main questions: 'Is an international democratic system possible among solely autocratic states?' and 'Is an international autocratic system possible among solely democratic states?' To both questions Bobbio provides a negative answer. His position is founded on the hypothesis that democratic regimes have a tendency to apply the principles which inform their domestic politics to the sphere of foreign affairs as well. However, this cannot always occur because democratic states have to function frequently in an autocratic international political environment. A third and related question should therefore be added: 'Can a state be fully democratic in a world that is not (as yet) democratic?'

The existence of a 'non-aggression pact' among all key domestic groups is, Bobbio maintains, a prerequisite for the complex coexistence typical of democratic systems within nations. The same principle applies to international society: democracy can inform relations among states only if the latter manage to regulate the use of force, i.e., move from an antagonistic to an agonistic spirit. Furthermore, the capacity of democracies to regulate domestic violence institutionally makes them more peaceful than autocracies in their relations with other states.

Many recent studies have considered how political regimes, and democratic systems especially, affect the foreign policy of states. Using quantitative methods, a large body of literature has taken into account the most easily measurable phenomenon of inter-state relations, the occurrence of war.[6] All the wars that have taken place since 1816 have been classified according to the type of political regime of the states involved. The conclusion of these studies is that, historically, democracies have not been more peaceful than autocracies at all. Not that this empirical result has sufficed to disavow the hypothesis that democracies base their foreign policies on a wholly different type of conduct from autocracies. The debate has since shifted to the subordinate hypothesis that, albeit as belligerent as autocracies, democracies tend not to fight among themselves. Historical and statistical analyses have in fact shown that wars between democracies are extremely rare and, when they do occur, are the result of extenuating circumstances.[7] In brief, a 'peace apart' has prevailed among democratic states, but it has in no way affected their stance towards autocracies. Moreover, whenever democracies have banded together against autocracies (as was the case in the two world wars), they have shown no scruples about allying with other autocratic regimes.

To date, the debate about democracies' propensity to war has hinged mainly on statistical analyses, and few attempts have been made to pursue the complex interpretive problems involved. The most immediate problem posed by the empirical data is: if democracies have been able to find non-violent ways of solving their disputes, why have they failed to apply the same procedures in connection with other types of state? The implicit answer is that wars between democracies and autocracies are caused because of the domestic regimes of the latter. The assumption is that, if all states were democratic, then the problem of war would disappear. And if war were eradicated, this would be a fundamental step towards a more elaborate society of nations which, in turn, would necessarily give rise to a democratic global system.

Despite the enormous amount of empirical research that has been carried out on the relationship between war and domestic political systems, very little research has been devoted to the legality and legitimacy of warfare. This is to a large extent owing to the difficulties involved in classifying wars as 'just' or 'unjust'. Following a substantially positivist approach, empirical research has confined itself to stressing one fact in particular: namely, that democracies do not fight each other. The largely unspoken, though sometimes openly expressed, assumption is that, when they do go to war, democracies do so because they are authorized to and, hence, behave justly. However, this deduction is not supported by studies showing that democracies only fight 'just wars': the interpretative issues are far more complicated.

Moreover, the theorem of 'peace among democracies' is a dangerous one. It almost suggests that by using any means to force autocratic regimes into submission, including war, the best of all possible worlds can be achieved: peace, legality, democracy. But since there are no international institutions authorized to ratify and safeguard international legality, this seems, at best, wishful thinking. In addition, this argument risks offering ideological ammunition to the strongest states – some of which owe their status precisely to their democratic systems – to defend their interests in the international realm regardless of the interests of weaker parties.

In short, an awareness that democracies do not fight one another does not relieve us of the responsibility to explore ways of creating democratic relations among nations. The achievement of democracy in the international community cannot be written off as a problem of domestic politics alone (see Chapter 2). Democracy has to be sought in the realm of inter-state relations as well.

Cosmopolitan Democracy

The title of this book, *Cosmopolitan Democracy*, refers to a system of geo-governance unlike any other proposed to date. We have deliberately chosen not to use the term 'international democracy' because we believe it is ambiguous. It can evoke a system of democratic rules and procedures among states without questioning the domestic constitution of the latter. Alternatively, it can conjure up a set of democratic systems with no extension of democratic values to inter-state relations. There are historic examples of both instances. On the one hand, there is the model of the Congress of Vienna which established wide-ranging inter-state consultative mechanisms, even though the majority of states concerned were, frankly, autocratic. On the other hand, there is the model of NATO, whose members are mainly democratic governments but whose procedures are by no means democratically based. The conception of world order invoked by cosmopolitan democracy is more ambitious than those covered by these instances. It takes as its aim the creation of a democratic community which both involves and cuts across democratic states.

The term *cosmopolitan* is used to indicate a model of political organization in which citizens, wherever they are located in the world, have a voice, input and political representation in international affairs, in parallel with and independently of their own governments. The conception of *democracy* deployed here is one that entails a substantive process rather than merely a set of guiding rules. For the distinctive feature of democracy is, in our judgement, not only a particular set of procedures (important though this is), but also the pursuit of democratic values involving the extension of popular participation in the political process.

Our point of departure is the simple observation that the states of the world today are quite different from one another, and that their diversity is reflected in their customs, cultures and political regimes. In order to defend the idea of a cosmopolitan democracy, it is necessary, first, to appreciate the anthropological diversity of political communities. But this appreciation does not mean that we have to accept the status quo uncritically, still less the principle of non-interference in the affairs of other states – a principle which has so often inspired the foreign policies (or non-policies) of democracies.

According to the cosmopolitan model, a more demo-cratic form of inter-state organization can be envisaged despite the diversity of domestic regimes; and its mapping need not be postponed to an unknown future when all members of the international community have reached a certain threshold of 'democracity'. This is the case for at least two reasons. First, the conception of democracy as a process concerns, albeit at very different levels, all countries. The entrenchment of democracy can start with the most elemental civil and political rights, while more developed democratic systems can always be deepened further. Second, an increase in the extent and scope of democracy within countries depends on increasing the accountability of the world order itself. Unless the world order becomes more democratic, democracy will always be restricted, delimited – if not thwarted – within nations.

Cosmopolitan democracy aims at a parallel development of democracy both within states and among states. This in turn requires the creation of authoritative global institutions able to monitor the political regimes of member countries and to influence the domestic affairs of states where necessary (some of the proposals to create these institutions are discussed by Daniele Archibugi in Chapter 5). But unlike many federalist projects, cosmopolitan democracy seeks neither to abolish existing states nor to replace their powers with an entirely different institutional framework. States must continue to perform their own administrative duties – at least until a new, demonstrably more effective form of political organization is invented (if it ever is). What is necessary is to deprive states of some of their more coercive and restrictive powers: in the former case, those powers which are deployed against the welfare and safety of citizens; in the latter case, those powers which are deployed to forestall or inhibit collaborative relations among states on pressing transnational questions. Cosmopolitan institutions must come to coexist with the established powers of states, overriding them only in certain, well-defined spheres of activity. It would not be the first time that established public power, i.e., national sovereignty, has been limited. During the Cold War, for instance, the USA and USSR dominated international affairs, while many states were often reduced to the role of onlooker. By contrast, cosmopolitan democracy envisages the limitation of national sovereignty by the direct intervention of democratic publics, or by what Richard Falk has dubbed 'the nascent global civil society' (see Chapter 6).

The programme for a cosmopolitan democracy has by no means appeared out of the blue. Numerous attempts have already been made to deprive states of some of the powers they have centralized and monopolized. The setting up of the United Nations and, even more so, the Universal Declaration of Human Rights have sought to guarantee the rights of the world's citizens irrespective of their belonging to one state or another. Since then, numerous solemn declarations have been passed by the United Nations, and many have subsequently been approved by the states themselves. Alas, these declarations have tended to be rhetorical rather than an expression of commitment to a wide set of positive rights. This has happened, first, because the desire to enforce human rights – if only through the formation of an autonomous Human Rights Court – has been weak and, secondly, because citizens have become possessors of such rights without corresponding executive, judicial and legislative powers.

If the contradictions of the international system are to be addressed – and its turbulence contained – new organizations and institutions will have to be established. In this volume, this is a vision linked directly to the creation and entrenchment of political bodies which would enable the peoples of the world, at diverse levels, to express and deliberate upon their aims and objectives in a progressively more interconnected global order. Such organizations would not draw their authority from the 'reason of arms' but, rather, from the 'arms of reason'. They might even be the germ for a secular process, transforming politics from a mode of domination to a mode of service. This and this alone is the political programme of cosmopolitan democracy, sketched in the chapters which follow.

NOTES

1   See David Held (ed.), *Prospects for Democracy: North, South, East, West* (Cambridge: Polity Press, 1993).

2   See David Held, 'Democracy, the Nation-State and the Global System', in D. Held (ed.), *Political Theory Today* (Cambridge: Polity Press, 1991).

3   Claus Offe, *Disorganized Capitalism* (Cambridge: Polity Press, 1985), pp. 286 ff.

4   For an account of these traditions, see Daniele Archibugi, 'Models of International Organization in Perpetual Peace Projects', *Review of International Studies*, 18 (1992), pp. 295–317; F. H. Hinsley, *Power and the Pursuit of Peace* (Cambridge: Cambridge University Press, 1963). In Chapter 2, Bonanate also calls attention to the English idealist school which was active between the two world wars.

5   Paradigmatic examples of a failure to analyse the conditions of democracy among nations include Raymond Aron, *Peace and War: A Theory of International Relations* (London: Weidenfeld & Nicolson, 1966); and R. J. Rummel, *Understanding Conflict and War*, Vol. 5: *The Just Peace* (Los Angeles: Sage, 1981).

6   See the pioneering work by Melvin Small and J. David Singer, *Resort to Arms, International and Civil Wars, 1816–1980* (Beverly Hills, CA: Sage, 1982).

7   One of the most perspicacious advocates of this thesis is Bruce Russett, *Grasping the Democratic Peace* (Princeton: Princeton University Press, 1993).

1

Democracy and the
International System

Norberto Bobbio

I

In recent years, I have addressed two of the 'great dichotomies' of general political theory: democracy–autocracy
and peace–war. Given my legally oriented academic background, I have addressed them mainly in terms of their
respective normative structures. The first can be reduced
normatively to the dichotomy of autonomy–heteronomy,
the second to that of *nomia*–anomy, which demonstrates
that the first is a subspecies of the second; in other words,
that democracy and autocracy are both forms of *-nomia* at
odds with a typically anomic situation such as war. The
question arises: what is the relationship between the two
nomic forms and the anomy of war? Is it the same for
both, or does it differ?

This question has raised a number of issues that have
been widely discussed by international relations scholars
over the last few years. They concern both the relationship
between domestic democracy and international peace and
the inverse relationship between international democracy
and domestic peace.[1] The whole debate stems from two
more radically opposed questions: 'Is an international
democratic system possible among solely autocratic
states?' and 'Is an international autocratic system possible

among solely democratic states?' They are formulated not because they need to be answered (the negative answer is automatic in both cases), but to highlight the web of problems which comparison of the two dichotomies creates. Those currently under discussion may be summarized roughly as follows. (1) Are democracies more peaceful than autocracies? (2) If they are, can external peace depend on the progressive increase in the number of democratic states and the democratization of the international community? (3) What are the consequences of the presence of non-democratic states in the international system and the non-democratization of the system itself for the domestic democracy of democratic states? In other words, is it possible to be fully democratic in a non-democratic world?

It is this last point which interests me most here. In recent studies, I have described the development of modern democracy in terms of the promises it has failed to keep[2] – in part, because they simply could not be kept, and, in part, due to unexpected obstacles. To date I have considered only domestic obstacles. I have yet to address the external obstacles that a democratic regime encounters in its role as a member of international society – which is *per se* essentially anomic and of which non-democratic states are also members.

In his last essay before his death, *Autoritarismo e democrazia nella società moderna* (Authoritarianism and Democracy in Modern Society), Gino Germani questioned whether democracies will survive in the future. Among the causes of the vulnerability of democracies with respect to autocracies, Germani also considered the external causes that depend on the relations which each state inevitably has with others. His conclusion was that, 'in the present state of the "international system", the situation of close interdependence and the internationalization of domestic politics tend to favour authoritarian as opposed to democratic solutions.'[3] In *Comment les démocra-*

cies finissent (Paris: Grasset, 1983), Jean-François Revel argues, with customary forcefulness and polemical rigour, that democracies are bound to come to an end, that they will represent no more than a brief episode in the history of the world because of their inability to defend themselves from their great enemy, totalitarianism. This is, he says, due in part to domestic dissent and in part to excessive compliance towards their more astute, ruthless antagonist. Richard Falk, director of the Centre of International Studies at the University of Princeton, argues that, 'even if a nuclear war does not break out, the existence of nuclear arms is in fundamental contrast with a democratic system.'[4]

These are only a few of the many examples that might be cited of the connection which has been revealed and described in recent years between democracy and the international system. It may now be interesting to explore the limits placed by domestic affairs on a democratic state in its international relations as a member of a system of mostly non-democratic states with a non-democratic constitution (supposing of course that we can speak of an international constitution as we speak of a domestic constitution).

II

History repeats itself – as do our reflections about it. The republican writers who survived the formation of the great monarchies argued more or less the same thesis as they watched republics being subjugated by their more powerful neighbours. Just as the liberty of the cities of ancient Greece was brought to an end by the Macedonian conquests, so European liberty, identified with the history of the free communes, also came to an end. Luckily, it is not only ideas which repeat themselves, but also erro-

neous forecasts. The end of the eighteenth century was to
see the birth of the United States, the greatest republican
state since the end of the Roman republic, a fact which
belied all previous lamentations about the end of republics. Perhaps the prophets of doom were about to be
proved wrong once again?

Republican theory never died in eighteenth-century
Britain, Holland, Italy and France, even though the great
territorial states entered the modern era as monarchies. It
had always attributed republican states, even aristocratic
republics, with a greater desire for peace than the great
monarchic states. Republics, it was said, were better at
the art of commerce than at the art of war. In the *Memoirs*
of Jan de Witt, which open with the motto *Sola respublica
veram pacem et felicitatem experitur*, the desire for the well-
being of republics is at odds with the desire for power and
expansion of monarchies: hence, 'the inhabitants of a
republic are infinitely happier than the subjects of a
country governed by a single supreme leader.' Whereas
the political art of princes had been compared to the
strength of the lion and the cunning of the fox (in one of
the most famous chapters in Machiavelli's *The Prince*), de
Witt compared the art of republics to the stealth of the cat,
which has to be both 'agile and prudent'.[5]

The thesis that republics are less warlike than monarchies was reiterated and consolidated by Montesquieu,
who argued with customary solemn peremptoriness that
the spirit of monarchies is war and the desire for great-
ness, while that of republics is peace and moderation. He
offered various justifications for his assertion: it is against
the nature of things, he said, for a republic to conquer a
city unwilling to enter its sphere; if a democracy conquers
a people to govern it as a subject, it endangers its own
liberty since it will be forced to confer excessive authority
on the magistrates it despatches to the conquered state.
Precisely inasmuch as they are weaker, republics had

always displayed a tendency to join together in permanent confederations or leagues, like the cities of ancient Greece and, later, the United Provinces of Holland and Swiss cantons. Once more, it was against the nature of things for one state to conquer another within the context of a federal constitution. In this respect, republics not only offered an example of reduced aggressiveness, they also generated the permanent alliances and associations among states which Montesquieu described so enthusiastically as 'societies of societies'. These associations, which made their appearance in the first perpetual peace projects, such as Kant's, have represented a *sine qua non* for the pursuit of a permanent peace policy ever since.

III

That the majority of states existing in the world today are not democratic is unquestionable. All we can do is take stock of the fact. The point deserves some attention, though, for in what sense and why cannot international society today be said to be democratic? I believe that the best way to answer the question is by describing the birth process of a democratic government as it was rationally reconstructed by seventeenth- and eighteenth-century contractarian doctrines. Their point of departure is the state of nature, the anomic state mentioned above, which still survives in international relations as a state of permanent – if not actual, potential – war. Their point of arrival is the civil state, seen as a state of if not perpetual at least stable peace. The shift from the one to the other is the result of an agreement or set of agreements, the first of which is a non-aggression pact – undeclared, tacit or implicit – among the single individuals who wish to emerge from the state of nature.

Like any other pact, the non-aggression pact is defined

by its content,[6] which, albeit purely negative and not explicitly mentioned in the works of the contractarians, is of the utmost importance for the birth of civil society. It consists of the reciprocal commitment of the contracting parties to exclude the use of violence from their relations. This commitment is in perfect antithesis to relations among individuals and groups in the state of nature, in which there is no rule to exclude – hence to disqualify as illegitimate – the use of violence. Although the existence of natural laws – 'do not kill' first and foremost – is presupposed, there is no pact which ensures their observance. Insofar as it is merely negative, the non-aggression pact is only the premise for the establishing of civil society.

On the basis of a second, positive pact, the contracting parties agree to establish rules for the peaceful solution of future conflicts. To use the terminology of Julien Freund,[7] this second pact marks the passage from the polemical state to the agonistic state; that is, from the situation characteristic of the state of nature, in which conflicts are resolved solely by force and the only law is so-called club law, to the new situation in which subjects exclude the use of reciprocal force to resolve conflicts, undertaking to settle them by negotiation, which leads by necessity to compromise. The passage from the polemical state to the agonistic state is not tantamount to a passage to a non-conflictual state: what changes is the way in which conflicts are resolved. And it is precisely this way which makes the difference, as far as the civil process is concerned. Other no less important innovations are introduced later, but the real improvement in standards coincides with the prohibition of the recourse to reciprocal violence as a means of upholding one's reasons.

What follows immediately afterwards springs from the consideration that both negative and positive pacts may, in turn, be violated. If it is to be peremptorily valid, the prohibition of the recourse to reciprocal force must hold even when the non-aggression pact and the subsequent pact based on the pledge not to resort to force are not observed. In other words, the ban on the recourse to reciprocal violence must be valid for the solution of not only secondary conflicts, but also the primary conflict that may arise from non-observance of the original non-aggression pact. At which point it is necessary to make a further step forward. To prevent the force that has been forbidden for the settling of secondary conflict from being used to resolve primary conflict, the only solution available is the intervention of a Third Party, of a figure (either collective or individual) distinct from the contracting parties. Since we are retreading – albeit with a few extra stages – the course marked out by natural law theorists in their reconstruction of state power, it is worth considering the importance assumed by the figures of the Arbitrator and the Judge in the passage from state of nature to civil state as described by Hobbes and Locke in their respective political theories.

IV

The passage from the polemical state to the agonistic state may be redefined as a passage from a situation without a Third Party to one with a Third Party. This latter situation is the final stage in the process, since an improvement in standards has already taken place with the non-aggression pact, which does not necessarily imply the presence of a Third Party. This presence is, as a legal scholar might say, required not so much to make the pact valid as to make it effective, although it is worth pointing out that its validity may, in the final analysis, depend on its effectiveness. In the polemical state, only two Third Party figures can be taken into consideration: the Ally (as Hobbes predicted, although this is clearly only an apparent Third Party, since the Ally is he who chooses one side or another, but does not help to transform the situation from dyadic into triadic by his presence) and the Neutral (he who sides with neither of the two contenders but is a Third Party totally removed from the conflict, whether it takes place according to the logic of the polemical or the agonistic state). The Neutral thus deserves to be termed the passive Third Party.

Only in the agonistic state does the active Third Party appear. This is the Third Party who intervenes directly in the resolution of the conflict. In other words, according to varying degrees of involvement and responsibility, it is on him that the resolution of the conflict depends. The first active Third Party figure is the Mediator, who brings the first two parties into contact, but does not replace them in the pursuit of a solution. The second is that of the Arbitrator, to whom the parties delegate a decision, undertaking to subscribe to it. The third is the Judge, who is authorized to intervene to resolve conflict from a higher level, and hence fully deserves to be acknowledged as a *super partes* Third Party.

At the moment in which the Judge appears, the agonistic state has already changed into another form of state, which we might define as a pacific state in contrast with the polemical state. The pacific state is born of the pact which the natural law scholars used to call *pactum subiectionis*, on the basis of which the parties in conflict submit to a common authority, who receives the right, among others, to designate a supposedly impartial *super partes* judge to establish who is right and who is wrong. Rather than Freund's dichotomy, I prefer the trichotomy according to which the agonistic state is an intermediate stage between two extremes: the state of nature and the civil state. Natural law scholars fully recognized the complexity and graduality of the process, distinguishing the *pactum societatis*, which corresponds to the agonistic state, from the *pactum subiectionis*, which corresponds to the state which, after Hobbes, I have termed pacific. To be more precise, it is necessary to distinguish two different Judge figures: one who, despite his superior authority, does not have the coercive power to enforce his decision (as still happens in international law today) and another whose superior authority grants him this power insofar as the pact of obedience has entrusted the use of legitimate force to it and it alone. Only in this latter stage is the pacific state wholly achieved. In reality, between the agonistic state and the pacific state there is an intermediate transition stage: that of the powerless Judge. There is also a transition stage between the purely polemical and agonistic states when the apparent and passive Third Party figures first appear on the scene.

I repeat, the decisive event in the emergence from the state of nature is the initial non-aggression pact according to which the parties dispense with the use of reciprocal force. Paradoxically, the ultimate purpose of the pact, to emerge from the state of war inherent in the state of nature, materializes only when the prohibition of the recourse to reciprocal force is guaranteed by the constitution – whether imposed or agreed upon – of a superior force.

Imposed or agreed upon? So far our argument has kept within the limits of the war–peace dichotomy. Now, however, we must turn our attention to another dichotomy, this time internal to civil society: that of democracy–autocracy. The passage from polemical state to pacific state is related to the formation of the state itself. Yet there can be different forms of state, democracy and autocracy representing the most opposed ideals. Remaining in the sphere of natural political philosophy's rational reconstruction, the distinction between these two ideals depends on the way in which we conceive the *pactum subiectionis*, be it conditional or unconditional, or, better still, on the diverse, more or less restrictive conditions with which coercive power – the power to use common force to avoid the use of reciprocal force – is devolved and acknowledged. Any democratic pact must include the following two conditions: (1) that sovereign power, exercised by anyone, including the contracting parties themselves, must not extend beyond the liberties and powers which individuals or groups have in the state of nature, and must thus respect those liberties and powers which, by virtue of their unassailability, are considered natural, hence unlimitable, unsuppressible rights; (2) that rules be established for collective decisions that are binding on the whole community, allowing such decisions to be taken with the highest level of participation and consent by the contracting parties themselves (if not unanimously, at least by a majority decision). In contrast, an autocratic pact is one in which sovereign power is instituted either without limits or solely with self-imposed limits, and collectively binding decisions are taken by a narrow power group or even by a single authority without the participation and consent of their recipients.

There may be historically intermediate forms between these two ideal types, but only by constructing the latter is it possible to understand the former. Likewise, the rational reconstruction has analytical and heuristic value even if it is at odds with real historical development, although we cannot rule out, of course, that, in some cases, history may indeed have followed this route. It may suffice to consider the way in which the present democratic Italian government was formed. During the internecine war provoked by the fall of a dictatorship following military defeat, anti-Fascist political groups immediately established a reciprocal non-aggression pact on the basis of which the force they had at their disposal was to be used against the common enemy, not in their potentially conflictual reciprocal relations. This pact gave rise to the

Committee of National Liberation, whose members subsequently reached an explicit agreement to establish rules
at the end of the war to allow them to resolve any further
disagreement peacefully. I need hardly add that, to date,
the formation and observance of the initial non-aggression
pact and the successive democratic pact is at the very base
of our civil coexistence, and that the legitimacy of our
political system continues to be founded on both.

V

On the basis of this rational reconstruction of the various
stages in the formation of a democratic state, we can
observe what has been happening for centuries and what
is still happening to a large extent in relations between
states within what, albeit euphemistically, we call the
international system. We inevitably note many
differences.

In the first place, in past centuries, if there was a non-
aggression pact at all among the subjects of international
society which made alliances with one another, it was
made only among a limited number of them. Even when
it was defined as 'Holy' or 'Grand', an alliance was always
a union limited in time and aims and, above all, in the
number of subjects who were a party to it. An alliance is
essentially a union of a group of states set up against
other states. All the earliest perpetual peace projects
proposed was a permanent, only hypothetically enduring
alliance among states which saw themselves as sharing
common interests. Only with the League of Nations (in
principle but not in fact) and with the United Nations (in
principle and, save for the odd exception, virtually in fact)
has the mutual non-aggression pact comprised, or tended
to comprise or claimed to comprise, all members of
international society.

In the second place, for centuries the only Third Party figure with which international society was acquainted was that of the Mediator or Arbitrator. This is a typical figure of the state which, no longer solely polemical, has become agonistic, but has still to turn into a pacific state according to my definition above. The Judge as a permanent, institutionalized, *super partes* arbitrator appeared on the scene only at the end of World War I, and subsequently reappeared after World War II with the creation of the International Court of Justice. Yet this continued to be a Judge whose decisions, unlike those of the judge in a state, cannot be enforced by recourse to exclusive rights of coercive power.

In the third place, in past centuries, whenever the anomic state failed, this happened not by agreement and the formation of confederations or federal states – corresponding respectively to *pactum societatis* and to the democratic *pactum subiectionis* – but through the imposition of one state or group of states over others. In other words, it assumed the form typical of autocratic power. This was especially true in recent centuries with the colonial expansion of the great European powers. Generally speaking, the history of international relations has so far registered either the anomic relationship or the autocratic relationship (that is, either anarchy or empire). Only with the League of Nations first, and the United Nations later, did it experience the third way, overriding anarchy without lapsing into autocracy or, using the concepts outlined above, achieving anomy without falling into heteronomy. The two basically universal institutions were a product of a veritable *pactum societatis*, which has yet to be followed by a *pactum subiectionis*, the submission of the various parties to a common authority endowed with exclusive rights of coercive power.

A great step forward has been made, as I said above, in terms of not only the universality of the pact, but also of its democratic inspiration. This is plain in the UN's recognition of human rights, which prejudicially limits the authority born of the agreement without endowing it with unlimited power comparable with that of autocratic governments. It is also clearly visible in its creation of an institution typical of any democratic society: the Assembly in which all contracting parties are equally represented and all decisions taken by a majority vote. I speak deliberately of democratic inspiration and not of democracy. In fact, with respect to the first point, save for the odd minor exception, guarantees of human rights in the international system cease at the threshold of the sovereign power of single states by virtue of the principle of non-intervention. With respect to the second point, moreover, the UN Assembly, founded on the democratic principle of political equality and regulated by the equally democratic principle of the majority, is flanked by the Security Council, each of whose five permanent members has the right of veto on non-procedural questions. Finally, and most important of all, international democracy is incomplete because the democratization process has stopped at society; it has yet to reach the political level, and if and when it ever will is unclear. This is an important point because the political level is the one at which not only society but also the state is democratic in the sense in which, speaking of domestic relations, we say that a government is democratic as opposed to autocratic.

VI

It is worth making a few observations here on the effect of this blockage on the democratization process at the very moment in which inter-state society is transformed into infrastate society ('infrastate' in the sense that the society of citizens in a single state is infrastate). The decisive power ratios, which determine the moves of the society of states and transformations in the overall system of the members of that society, continue to be those between great powers. Until very recently they were embodied substantially in relations between just two such powers; so much so, that it was plausible to interpret the system as bipolar. The relations that existed between the two great powers were those typical of any system of reciprocal equilibrium. They were identical to the relations that had existed between great powers for centuries before the start of the process of universalization and democratization which was set laboriously into motion after World War I, and carried forward with some improvements following the interruption caused by World War II. The relations between the real subjects of the international system were once defined as the 'balance of power', while for decades following World War II they were defined as the 'balance of terror'. All that had changed was that the power of arms had increased, not altered, the reason for the balance, which was and continues to be reciprocal fear.

Reciprocal fear is the characteristic of the Hobbesian state of nature. It determines instability, insecurity and vulnerability; it is, in short, responsible for all those drawbacks which persuade man to emerge from this particular state and to found a society with a common authority. The passage from state of nature to civil state is the passage from a state of unstable equilibrium – in which each individual is afraid of each and all others – to a state of stable order founded on the existence of a common authority whose main duty is to deliver each of the members of the new society from reciprocal fear. As long as a situation of inter-individual relations is characterized by reciprocal fear, it is a state of nature situation, one in which security is unstable, and which individuals seek to leave by any means. The principal means is the

institution of a common authority. Of course the purely
hypothetical situation of the universal state of nature is
entirely different from that of a few or only two parties.
However, when a few or only two parties hold the greater
power and do not yield to the authority of a superior
Third Party, the relationship between them ultimately
dominates the system as a whole, fostering despotic
relations within the power system of each. Both anarchy
between equals and despotism between unequals obstruct
the process of democratization of the system, which is the
only way to emerge from anarchy without stumbling into
despotism or, inversely, to dissolve a despotic system
without stumbling into anarchy.

In contemporary international relations, the traditional
system of equilibrium between more than one power or
groups of powers and the new system launched by the
democratization process continue to live side by side. The
new system has yet to eliminate the old one completely
because it has failed to create a strong common authority.
At the same time, the survival of the old has not strangled
the new, but by depriving it of power has prevented it
from achieving its ends. The contrast between the two
systems can also be viewed in terms of the distinction,
familiar to legal scholars, between legitimacy and effectiveness. The new system is made legitimate by the tacit
or express consent of the majority of members of the
international community which gave life to – and continues to keep alive – the United Nations to which, one
by one, newly formed states have adhered. Yet it has
scant effectiveness. The old continues to be effective even
though it has lost all legitimacy with respect to the letter
and the spirit of the United Nations Statute. It is arduous
today to forecast which of the two systems will eventually
prevail.[8]

Albeit with differing degrees of intensity, this contrast
between legitimacy and effectiveness is also visible inside

democratic governments. Here the system of legal relations clashes continuously with that of real relations;
hence democratic governments vary greatly according to
the intensity of the contrast. The real power of a large-
scale multinational firm challenges legitimate democratic
government in the same way in which a great power
shuns UN resolutions or a decision by the Hague Court of
Justice. We often hear, even at the domestic level, of the
'double-state' system.[9] By this we mean that, alongside
the system envisaged by the constitution, in which collective decisions must be taken by competent bodies according to pre-established procedures, a new system has
developed whereby many collective decisions are taken
directly by the groups concerned through agreements
founded exclusively on the recognition of reciprocal
power. Hence we speak of a dual international system
composed of two conceptually incompatible systems
which are aware of, but do not recognize, each other,
which do not ignore each other but act independently of
each other.

VII

The possible consequence of this state of affairs on the
domestic order of democratic states was suggested by my
initial question: 'Can a state be fully democratic in a world
that is not (as yet) democratic?' The only way to solve this
type of problem is by analysing the ways in which the
domestic system is affected by the international system,
and by establishing which of these influence the democratic system directly.

For the time being, I shall simply make a few preliminary observations on the general issue of the relations
between domestic and international order. This is often
framed as a dilemma: does the first have primacy over the

second or vice versa? Let me say straightaway that, put this way, the question is virtually unanswerable. I do believe, however, that it is possible to offer a significant reply on the specific issue of the limits imposed on a domestic democratic system by the context in which it finds itself. It is necessary to remember that not all states are democratic and the democratization process has yet to be completed. I repeat, by 'democratic state' I mean a state founded on a non-aggression pact among different political groups and on their stipulation of a set of rules permitting the peaceful solution of any conflict that may arise among them. I repeat also that the principal effect of the unfinished process of democratization of the international order is that, in the final analysis, the only way of resolving conflicts that arise in the international system is by recourse to reciprocal violence. This is a result both of the ineffectiveness of the universal non-aggression pact underlying the UN Charter and of the relative effectiveness of the non-aggression pacts stipulated among states with clear defence–offence intentions *vis-à-vis* other groups of states. There is no shortage of examples of the phenomenon in the contemporary world; they range from the Iran–Iraq conflict to that between Israel and the Arab states. Even the great conflict between the two superpowers – the non-solution of which complicated the peaceful solution of all other minor conflicts – was the consequence of a mortal dispute whose temporary postponement depended exclusively on the threat of reciprocal force.

In a world among whose members an effective, universal non-aggression pact is impossible, aggression is possible at any moment. Albeit condemnable and often condemned by the laws in force, such aggression is invariably unpunishable and unpunished. If this is the case, the supreme principle on which a state bases its conduct is the principle of survival – which is exactly what happens in the Hobbesian state of nature. The principle has a classical formulation in the Ciceronian maxim 'Salus populi suprema lex esto' (*De legibus*, III, 3), which has been repeated with only a few variants down the centuries. Let us now try to apply this maxim to the domestic situation of a democratic government founded on a non-aggression pact among the various (political) parties. Let us imagine that one of these declares, 'The supreme law is the safety of the party.' A false note is immediately audible. The maxim would sound less off-key in a context in which there were no 'constitutionalized' non-aggression pact among the various parties; this is the case among parties at loggerheads during civil wars, or in the permanent civil war which was fought in the cities of ancient Greece or in medieval communes. Here, each political group or faction managed to attain power only through the use of violence. In the present international system, the great powers in particular often replace the old maxim with an appeal to 'vital interests', but the meaning does not change. Their aim is to protect the ultimate value implicit in the 'salus' concept, which, in conformity with the principle 'the end justifies the means', legitimizes any action subordinated to that end, however morally wrong or unlawful it may be.

For a moral legitimation of actions performed in the state of necessity or exception in which all states – hence democratic states too – find themselves in a system in which threat and use of reciprocal force are the rule, one need go no further than Machiavelli's argument, considered one of the cornerstones of reason of state theory:

> For when the safety of one's country wholly depends on the decision to be taken, no attention should be paid either to justice or injustice, to kindness or cruelty, or to its being praiseworthy or ignominious. On the contrary, every other consideration being set aside, that alternative should be wholeheartedly adopted which will save the

life and preserve the freedom of one's country. (*Discourses*, III, 41)

Here, 'every other consideration being set aside' means setting aside all respect for those values which make a domestic order a civil order – first and foremost, for the value of the liberty of citizens.

When we speak of the 'salus populi' principle, the distinction between democratic and non-democratic governments is irrelevant. Conclusive proof of the fact comes with the European Convention of Human Rights, stipulated among democratic states. In its first articles, it lists the traditional rights of freedom which recur in the bills of rights upon which liberal states are based. But in article 15 it introduces the principle of the state of exception, proclaiming that, 'In time of war or other public emergency threatening the life of the nation, any High Contracting Party may take measures derogating from its obligations under this Convention'. Of the many justifications that have been made for the distinction between morality and politics, and that have constituted the body of reason of state doctrine, the one most frequently used has been that of 'derogation'. There is no general law which does not allow derogations in exceptional cases. What is not allowed in domestic relations, which are presumed to be founded on a hierarchical relationship of command–obedience between rulers and ruled, is allowed in a system of sovereign states in which, at least at a certain level, there is no command–obedience relationship and the security of each depends uniquely on its capacity of self-defence (which of course also comprises preventive attack).

The state of effective war, which really is exceptional, cannot be compared with the state of permanent insecurity in which every state finds itself in a system, such as the international one, in which there is no common authority, no Third Party above all others endowed with sufficient coercive power. Nor must we overlook the difference between this state of insecurity and the state of greater or relative security in which, barring major constitutional crises, a government generally finds itself domestically. It is precisely by bearing in mind this difference that we can understand the ways in which domestic policy may be affected by foreign policy. In the case of a democratic government, they are clear in its difficulty or inability to observe the same commitments in foreign policy as it undertakes, and is, moreover, able to maintain, in domestic policy.

VIII

One such commitment is to render power visible. The distinguishing feature of democracy – upon which I have never ceased to insist in recent years[10] – is that of the publicity of government records. Only when a record becomes public are citizens in a position to judge it, and hence to exercise one of the fundamental prerogatives of any citizen in a democracy: the control of his rulers. At the dawn of representative democracy, Guizot, the author of *Histoire des origines du gouvernement représentatif* (1821–2), wrote that the publicity of debates in the chamber of representatives compelled the authorities to pursue justice and reason in full public view to convince each and every citizen of their good faith. The principle of visibility is a revolutionary one because it resists the natural tendency of power – of every form of power – to hide itself, either by not declaring its intentions in public or by lying about them, thus withdrawing from the indiscreet gaze of the people, or by masking (and camouflaging) itself. Like God, the potentate tends to make himself inaccessible: the *arcana dominationis* are an imitation of the *arcana naturae* (or of the *arcana Dei*). Elias Canetti's memorable pages on 'secrecy' as the essence of power deserve to be meditated upon (as does his whole book *Crowds and Power*). Power must be as inscrutable as the decrees of God. By not being seen it has a better view of what others are doing: 'Power is impenetrable. The man who has it sees through other men, but does not allow them to see through him. He must be more reticent than anyone; no one must know his opinions or intentions.'[11]

Precisely because the principle of the visibility of power is unnatural, it is also the hardest to observe: power resists every attempt by its victims to flush it out, to force it into the open, to remove its mask – in short, to tell the truth. It always finds some pretext for not revealing itself; it always advances plausible arguments to justify its infringement of the obligation of transparency. The two commonest pretexts or arguments are, and have always been: (1) that affairs of state are too complicated to be divulged to the public, which would be unable to understand them anyway; (2) that it is wrong to let one's enemy know one's intentions. The recipients of these two government maxims are subjects and other states. Both – the second, especially – continue to reveal their binding force in foreign policy.

Beyond or below the sphere of public action, the violation of established rules may have consequences of a political nature – even if only in the form of the political discrediting of the perpetrator – and of a legal nature, in which case the extreme sanction is impeachment. Yet another part of political action takes place in an even more mysterious, inaccessible, unknowable sphere. This is the action of secret services, which is always tacitly accepted. Albeit subject to discussion or only to theoretical criticisms of no practical value, it is, by and large, regarded as legitimate even in democratic states. Kant resolutely denied the separation of politics from morality. Reading

the condemnation of the use of spies and any other secret
means of combat in wartime (and presumably all the more
so in peacetime) in his pamphlet *Towards Perpetual Peace,*
one cannot help smiling at the naïvety of a great philos-
opher who so obviously had his head in the clouds. The
sphere of application of all these forms of secret action is,
once more, mainly that of foreign policy; that is, of
relations between separate and potentially hostile political
subjects in a realm in which one of the consequences of
the inexistent or unfinished process of democratization
has been to prevent the full implementation of the principle of the visibility of power. The only way of fighting
invisible power is through equally invisible power: likewise, the only way of countering secrecy is through
secrecy itself. If anything, contenders will end up squab-
bling over who has the most effective secret service, the
most reliable spies, the most guarded counter-espionage,
over who is the most devious, over who is the best at the
art of lying and fraud, and so on.

IX

I am well aware that my whole argument is based on
conjecture inspired by the Kantian idea that perpetual
peace is feasible only among states with the same form of
government – republican government (the form in which
collective decisions are made by the people) – supplemented by the idea that the union of all states must
also be republican in form. I also realize that such conjecture cannot be verified. As an idea of pure reason it is
valid in practice only insofar as it is regulative. Like any
conjecture, my thesis may be expressed only as an 'if-
then' hypothetic proposition: 'If all states were republican,
if the society of all states were republican, then . . .' 'If' is
the stumbling block. If the consequence is unverifiable

and unfalsifiable, the premise is improbable in the current international system. We are caught in one of those vicious circles in which every rational prediction breaks down. If it is possible to speak in terms of hope, then that hope is dependent exclusively upon the bounded nature, so often demonstrated, of our reason. The vicious circle may be formulated as follows: states can become democratic only in a fully democratized international society, but a fully democratized international society presupposes that all the states that compose it are democratic. The completion of one process is hindered by the non-completion of the other.

Be that as it may, the number of democratic states has continued to increase, and the process of the democratization of international society is now well and truly under way. This might suggest that the two tendencies do not hinder but rather corroborate one another in turn. It is still far too early, however, to transform a mere hope into a prediction.

Translated by John Irving

NOTES

1 For an introduction to this debate, see the anthology *Teoria e analisi nelle relazioni internazionali*, ed. L. Bonanate and C. M. Santoro (Bologna: Il Mulino, 1986).

2 I refer in particular to the first essay in my book *The Future of Democracy* (Cambridge: Polity Press, 1987).

3 In R. Scartezzini, L. Germani and R. Gritti (eds), *I limiti della democrazia* (Naples: Liguori, 1985), p. 34.

4 'Le armi nucleari e la fine della democrazia', in *I limiti della democrazia*, p. 295.

5 In F. Venturi, *Utopia e riforma nell'illuminismo* (Turin: Einaudi, 1970), pp. 35–6.

6 This non-aggression pact is the premise for all others. That

it happens hypothetically among natural individuals or, less hypothetically and more realistically, among natural groups such as the family, and hence that the contracting parties are not single individuals but group leaders, *patres familias*, has no particular relevance to the validity of the reconstruction. For Vico, who purports to replace the rational reconstruction of natural law theorists with a historical reconstruction – albeit referred to as an ideal history – of the birth of civil nations, the 'state of families' corresponds to the state of nature, and the union of heads of families corresponds to the civil state or, better still, to the first stage in civil society, which, he argues, gives rise to aristocratic republics. What is important for my argument is not the fact that, for Vico, the first stage in the historical course subsequent to the state of nature is the aristocratic republic and not the monarchic or democratic government, but that the passage from the state of nature to the civil state, from the state in which there is still no government to the state in which the first form of government appears, happens through a non-aggression pact among those – in this case, the *patres familias* – who intend to give life to a stable regime.

7 For this, and subsequent references to the topic of the Third Party, see P. P. Portinaro, *Il terzo: una figura del politico* (Milan: Franco Angeli, 1986), to which I am indebted for several ideas and suggestions.

8 The issue became topical once more during the period before and after the Gulf War, between the summer of 1990 and the spring of 1991. Contrasting interpretations have been made of the various UN Resolutions – from the first of 2 August 1990 (no. 660) to the last of 29 October 1990 (no. 672). Some saw UN intervention as proof that the process of formation of a common power *super partes* had come to a head, and therefore constituted an intermediate but already relatively significant stage in the passage from a situation of unstable equilibrium to one of more stable, collective security. According to others, the authorization of the use of force granted to the United States and their allies was new evidence of UN submission to the supremacy of a

great power and hence represented the passage from a situation of equilibrium to one of hegemony – not a step forward with respect to the process of formation of a common power, but a step backwards.

9   I refer in particular to F. Fraenkel, *Il doppio stato: contributo alla teoria della dittatura* (Turin: Einaudi, 1983), and to my introduction.

10 I first argued this in 'Democracy and invisible powers', now in my book *The Future of Democracy* (Cambridge: Polity Press, 1987), returning to the theme in my preface to *La strage: l'atto di accusa dei giudici di Bologna* (Rome: Editori Riuniti, 1986), pp. ix–xx. See also M. Brutti, 'Democrazia e potere invisibile', *Rinascita*, 42: 33 (1985), pp. 28–30, and, for a more detailed presentation, the paper 'Democrazia e segreto', in P. Fuis (ed.), *Il trattato segreto*, Proceedings of the conference held in Sassari and Alghero, 24–26 March 1988 (Padua: Cedam, 1990), pp. 16–31.

11 E. Canetti, *Crowds and Power*, trans. C. Stewart (Harmondsworth: Penguin, 1973), p. 341.

2

Peace or Democracy?

Luigi Bonanate

1 Introduction: One of the Paradoxes of Democracy

The world has lived for forty years or more totally under the influence of nuclear weapons. Since the latter are by their very nature uncontrollable by any democratic procedure,[1] it may sound naïve at best even to dare speak in terms of international democracy. However, the fact that democracy has yet to materialize on the international stage should not stop us from asking if and how it might be achieved – if not fully, at least in part.

It may be useful to compare the two realms of domestic and international politics; the sharply defined features of the former will, hopefully, offer us a better understanding of elements and aspects of the latter which we might otherwise neglect or not detect at all. More generally speaking, if we were to project three beams of light (the democratic *process* and its *control* plus *access*, the number of participants in the two functions) onto a screen (the idea of democracy) to see exactly how much democracy is operating in the world today, we would see that only in a minority of the states effectively active on the international scene is a truly democratic process under way. We would also be able to note that, in a growing number of cases, control is becoming more democratic and, finally, that access to international decision-making procedures is extremely broad, though still selective. If, until a very few years ago, only two states attended top-level political and military summits (admittedly, preceded and followed by seemingly never-ending NATO talks), modern economic summits now host seven, and in them the positions of Great Britain, Germany, France and Italy reflect those of the other eight EC member countries.

The nuclear strategy implemented by the world's most democratic states introduced a paradox to international political life. To safeguard their independence, they threatened to perpetrate the most undemocratic action of all – the destruction of humanity. Nevertheless, the contemporary international system is littered with procedures and rules based increasingly on a *concert* of subjects *representing* (sometimes by invitation, sometimes by extortion) a number of other states. Making due distinctions, this mechanism may be likened to the one at work in the so-called consociate democracies.

Perhaps we were right to accept the idea that all political life is too schizophrenic to permit a strong link between the quality of domestic politics and that of its international counterpart. Perhaps a state that is democratic at home can be authoritarian abroad, and a state that is despotic at home can implement a liberal foreign policy. Anyone who accepts this formulation does not need to be reminded that, in the past, statist schizophrenia was considered neither an evil nor an illness. It was regarded quite simply as the inevitable consequence of the diversity that exists between the two realms in which political life unfolds. Thus although the commonest answer to my initial question is, 'Yes, the idea that this schizophrenia exists is acceptable', its justification is never actually discussed. It is passively accepted as a natural fact without ever being subjected to critical scrutiny. Since the idea that there is no link between the domestic and external conduct of a single state appears unacceptable, I intend not only to explore the reasons why, but also to use more systematic analysis to reframe the whole problem – though not of course to solve it. I do not deny that my agenda also conceals a prescriptive purpose: to corroborate the thesis that states are not allowed to act as they wish (that is, as they feel 'compelled' to do), but that they too are duty-bound to formulate value judgements (which they apply in practice, when they decide upon the content of their actions). In short, I wish to demonstrate that the idea that international life is barred from the realm of moral judgement is unacceptable because it is ideological and simplistic. A state cannot be allowed to declare itself democratic if it implements an authoritarian, repressive foreign policy, just as the former Soviet Union could not be considered effectively socialist when it acted despotically abroad. In the final analysis, foreign policy is no more devoid of values than domestic policy.

In what follows I wish to explore, in particular, the hypothesis that peace is a precondition for international democracy, seen both as a characteristic of inter-state relations and as a prerequisite by which states ought to abide when they elaborate their foreign policies. I thus imagine that peace is not merely a material good and that peace breeds peace, as we generally like to think, but that it may indeed be harnessed to create an international climate of democracy. I shall also seek to present an example of the democratization process which might be activated by analysing criticisms of the so-called hegemonic stability theory.

My argument is once more divided into three parts. After establishing the relevance of the issue of international democracy (§2), I seek to clarify the relationship between peace and democracy (§3). I then go on to assess the future prospects of international democracy (§4) and, finally (§5), in search of the foundations of a normative theory of democracy, discuss the relationship between international democracy and justice.

2   A Neglected Episode: 'Idealists' and Democracy

One way of verifying the relevance of the idea of international democracy is by asking whether it has ever been seriously discussed before. Despite the scepticism which the question sometimes arouses, the answer is nonetheless an affirmative one. It is illuminating here to consider the way in which the problem was posed by the group of scholars described today in the field of international relations as the idealistic school, the very founders of international studies. This latter consideration ought to provide food for thought for those international theorists who in their uncritical research on the idea of power politics have betrayed their origins. The idealistic school of international relations theory came into being in British Fabian circles at the turn of the century. It thrived in the first thirty years of the new century only to wane gradually as the crisis leading up to World War II came to a head.

This is neither the time nor the place to reconstruct the history of the movement. Suffice it to recall that Fabian socialism was not only profoundly ingenuous but also, paradoxically, paternalistic in its approach to international politics. This much is evident in the position taken by George Bernard Shaw, one of the most famous Fabians of the time, on the Boer War. In his view, the war was an inevitable, albeit painful, step towards progress.[2] More generally speaking, the naïvety of the idealists overrode the valuable achievements of the so-called legal pacificism of the period – international tribunals, arbitration and so

on. It veered in fact towards the hypothesis of a veritable
international government. Leonard Woolf was even com-
missioned by the Fabian Society to write a 250-page study
on the subject.[3] Just a few years later, in the aftermath of
World War I, the setting up of the League of Nations
seemed almost to make this albeit contradictory and
limited idealistic utopia materialize. Although it failed as
an institution, the League was nonetheless the first ever
concerted attempt at 'world government'. Be that as it
may, what I most wish to stress here is that the period
from 1920 to 1935 or thereabouts was characterized by a
singular and, for the purposes of my argument, highly
interesting feature: namely the fact that throughout those
years the issue of international democracy was widely and
seriously discussed. A journal such as the *Political Quarterly*, first published in 1930, whose editorial committee
included the likes of John Maynard Keynes, Harold Laski,
W. Robson and Leonard Woolf himself (otherwise famous
– or indeed more so – as the husband of Virginia),
purported to address social and political reality from a
progressive standpoint. International democracy was thus
one of its most recurrent themes. The issue was raised in
the very first article, by Alfred Zimmern, of the very first
issue of the journal. Today Zimmern's scholarship is much
neglected, but it is worth remembering that, besides being
a militant pacifist and the first ever professor of international relations anywhere, he also wrote a seminal and
monumental history of the League of Nations, of which
he was a functionary for some years.[4]

There was of course a good deal of ingenuousness in
Zimmern's approach too. What interests me most here,
though, is its symbolic value as an example of the debate
that was raging at the time. Here is how Zimmern
formulated the problem of international order in the early
1920s: 'What was the effect of the war upon democracy?
. . . It carried to completion the work of the English and

French Revolutions and made democracy, if not the sole, at least the normal and orthodox form of government throughout the European continent.'[5] Four years later, Viscount Cecil (winner of the Nobel Peace Prize in 1937) states in an essay that, even if the point of departure of international relations is natural inequality among individuals, the spirit of the League of Nations demands that each state receive the same consideration and treatment as others. This is tantamount to saying that 'the principle of democracy is implicit in the League',[6] which, since it works on the basis of the principle of unanimity (typical of any direct democracy), ultimately proves to be much more democratic than the various 'democratic' (*sic*!) states, burdened as they are by the difficulties involved in making their parliamentary institutions work with the majority principle. In other words, whenever the two function in the same way, international democracy is more complete than domestic democracy.[7] Cecil also appeals to the democratic role which world public opinion can perform and to the democratic control which populations must exercise over the foreign policies of their respective countries.[8] My third and last example is D. Thomson's essay, written three years later, devoted to the consideration that the League of Nations is, 'in the final analysis, the projection into the international sphere of the tolerant, secular state which was born at the Renaissance, and reached adolescence in the seventeenth, and maturity in the two successive centuries.'[9] It is to this consideration that Thomson traces the idea that the international system in which the League of Nations operates is basically nothing other than a product of the liberal democracy that had already developed in the world, and that it is indeed the 'apotheosis' of this type of state (p. 40).

It is easy to be ironic about such guileless visionaries. It would be unfair, however, not to explore the foundation of their reflections. We must first of all acknowledge that they were faced by a completely new international situation. The years preceding had been largely peaceful; the Briand–Kellogg Pact had evoked emotion and approval and the rising Fascist and Nazi regimes had yet to prove all their ultimately dire consequences. International conferences were also developing, especially those on disarmament and/or weapon control. Such events had no real historical precedent. We cannot let this fact pass, especially if we consider that the examples I have brought to light reflect initial (albeit crude) attempts to embrace a problem which inasmuch as it was virgin territory, possessed some elements of originality.

Not that I wish to act as the counsel for the defence of idealistic thinking: I simply wish to use it to demonstrate the relevance of the debate on international democracy. The arguments advanced by Zimmern, Cecil and Thomson may sound naïve to us, but they do have a certain intrinsic validity, if considered in terms of the relationship which inevitably exists between the development of the state as an institution and that of the interdependence of states. This was a highly original new dimension in the years in question. Only since then has it been possible to begin actually to formulate the problem in hand. The fact is that the discovery of the international nature of political life is a phenomenon typical of the twentieth century. It may have been possible for states to slip through its net in the past, but today this is out of the question. Which is why I not only invoke the school of thought which first came to terms with this innovation, but also stress its normative scope. In short, the idealists consciously, albeit somewhat unrealistically, were the first to pose the problem of the construction of an international democracy founded no longer on the sum total of domestic democracies, but on the very nature of international relations.

I thus feel more than justified in rehabilitating Leonard Woolf's last attempt, in 1940, to defend idealistic theory:

all the more so in view of the peremptoriness of his argument, a counter-deduction against those 'realists' who saw the outbreak of war as proof of the vainness of pacifism.[10] In his polemical essay 'Utopia and Reality', in which the chosen target is E. H. Carr, who had just published his forceful critique of idealistic theory, *The Twenty Years' Crisis*,[11] Woolf simply reverses the classical anti-international argument according to which international anarchy is the root of all evil. He asks instead whether the reason for the war which has just broken out may be sought not in the natural impossibility of peace, but rather in the lack of commitment by single states to achieve it. War is not the outcome of a crisis in the international system, but of the defeat suffered by regimes in which democracy has been replaced by dictatorship, parliamentary procedure by street violence, and in which purges, pogroms and mass imprisonment have become accepted means of administration.[12] In short, do the roots of world war lie in the inability of the League of Nations to perform its task or in the authoritarianism that was developing in the world? Did the League of Nations fail because of intrinsic weaknesses or because of extrinsic reasons for which it cannot be held responsible?

Woolf's argument is so obvious as to make any comment on my part superfluous. Yet it would be wrong to dismiss it as mere rhetoric. Incurably optimistic as it may sound to us, it provides the pivot for my whole argument. It is true that international theorists (and among them Woolf) claim the relative autonomy of international political life, rejecting the formulation according to which it is nothing more than the sum total of the foreign policies of states. Yet we cannot conceal the fact that no structure in the world can survive attacks launched from the inside. A car is the sum of a number of parts which combine to produce motion. Can we blame it if it fails to stop at a sudden obstacle when its brakes are faulty? If we consider the very nature of international life and the type of order with which it is acquainted (determined by the outcome of great constitutive wars which establish who will govern the international system and who will be compelled to obedience), it is easy to see why the outbreak of a subsequent war is hardly ever to be attributed to the prevailing 'government', and almost always to attempts by other states to make that government fall. How can we blame the system for the actions of one of its constituent parts? In other words: are we to penalize the international system for its alleged inability to exercise stringent, total control over the domestic affairs of single states? How can we expect a dimension of political reality whose autonomy we do not as a rule recognize to make its reasoning prevail over the sphere of autonomy of the state?

Woolf's critique might be reformulated in the question 'To what extent do single states commit themselves to the development of a peaceful international society?' Supposing that there are no natural reasons to prevent them from doing so, why shouldn't states be expected to assume their external responsibilities? Why shouldn't they contribute to the defence of international peace? It was not the failure of the League of Nations which provoked the world crisis but, on the contrary, the crisis which dragged the League of Nations in its wake. Yet Woolf's passionate public defence of the League of Nations also prompts reflection on the chronic difficulties we encounter when it comes to analysing international problems. Although the latter are invariably viewed through a state-centric lens, the blame for them is laid on the nature of international life (as if, considered as the mere consequence of the existence of states, it were blessed with autonomy of its own). But the real blame lies with the lack of good will or even downright hostility shown by states at war with each other. All of which further highlights the need to devote much greater attention to the relationship between the nature of domestic political regimes and that of international political regimes. It is important, for example, to understand how far a change in domestic regime can affect the durability of the international regime. The fact that Fascist and Nazi dictatorships replaced more or less democratic bourgeois parliamentary regimes is by no means without relevance to international political analysis. Likewise, unless we have a clearer, more conscious image of the international system (and hence of its regimes), it is impossible to understand the role of it in wars, what their purpose is and why states wage them – unless of course we consider them natural events independent of human will.[13]

3 Peace and Democracy

Now that we have struck a few healthy polemical blows for the cause of the international political problematic, we come to the heart of the matter, the relationship between peace and international democracy. This may be addressed from two different viewpoints. The first is based on the hypothesis that the democratic regime is, *per se*, non-violent and that peace among states will be possible only when all states become democratic (which seems to me to be the view of Doyle and Bobbio).[14] The second reverses the formulation: it argues that it is not democracy which fosters peace but that, vice versa, only the development of international peace can foster the diffusion of democracy.[15]

The first formulation is founded on acceptance of what I describe as the 'anything or nothing' saving clause: either all states reach the democratic stage equally and contemporaneously and hence produce absolute peace, or else – if just one state fails to cross this threshold – international democracy becomes impossible. Even if the

dream of equal democracy for all states were to materialize, some difficulties would remain nonetheless. To cite
just one example, this type of solution would continue
to be inadequate from the federalist standpoint (which is
not *per se* anti-democratic). According to this view, the
programme described would be useless simply because
the 'evil' lies within the state as such, not in one type
of regime as opposed to another. In the words of one of
the fathers of federalism, 'republics in practice have not
been less addicted to wars than monarchies'.[16] And what
can be said of the period which precedes the success of
universal democracy? If we continue to reason according
to the point of view outlined above, it follows that, as long
as undemocratic states exist, war will continue to be
possible (indeed, probable), and that the pursuit of a
democratic foreign policy may prove harmful even for
the most sincerely democratic state. If we add to this
the consideration that undemocratic foreign policies have
often been freely developed even by democratic states
(US policy towards Vietnam is one example), then we
must resign ourselves to the fact that this first path leads
us nowhere.

Yet if domestic democracy is unlikely to produce external peace, won't the reverse be true – as our second
hypothesis suggests? Isn't it peace which leads to international democracy? At first sight, one might be inclined
to answer in the affirmative. One might, that is, hypoth-
esize that if all states were, at a certain moment, to be
satisfied with an existing peace, then democratic relations
might effectively develop among them. But that answer is
plainly abstract and unrealistic: for, by definition, every
historical peace – the tangible outcome of a prior conflict –
inevitably dissatisfies the vanquished state or states.

Which is why the second point of view cannot solve the
problem either. That being said, however, it does seem to
me more acceptable than the first. At which point it may

be useful to analyse further the significance of the 'international democracy' formula. Let us suppose a hypothetical situation of international peace, irrespective of what
its effective content may be. Here again we are faced by
two different logics. If international democracy is an end
and an ideal, then in international relations it is embodied
in the peace that would prevail if all controversies among
states were to cease. This alas, leads us back into the
realm of the abstract. It is also possible for states to come
to an agreement over the rules to resolve their controversies peacefully (this, basically, was the dream of the
League of Nations). Albeit somewhat outmoded, this
position nonetheless suggests the possibility of a definition of international democracy with, as in domestic
democracy, an essentially procedural content. So what
should a democratic international system really be like? It
should, in the first instance, envisage equality among
states. Alas, states are, by nature, unequal (in nature they
do not exist at all), and the differences among them are
much more conspicuous than those among citizens. A
democratic international system should, secondly, be able
to generate a turnover of rulers: this, after all, is what
happens in the state through elections, and in the international system through wars. It should, thirdly, be
allowed to express dissent, and to form world public
opinion. The system, finally, ought to be equipped with
tools to allow it to resolve controversies and conflicts
peacefully whenever they arise.[17]

Faced with such an idyllic, unreal model, what effective
conduct can the state – the democratic state – assume in
its foreign policy? In other words, what is the significance
of a state's conducting itself democratically in its relations
with the outside world? Has a democratic state to
implement a democratic foreign policy and an authoritarian state an authoritarian one? Not necessarily: the United
States, as we have seen, quite often carries out external

actions that are by no means democratic. The Soviet
Union, in turn, conducted itself in an objectively democratic way when it implemented a pro-decolonization
policy within the UN. Both types of state may, therefore,
behave incoherently!

This is no great revelation (nor does it really deserve
the space I have reserved to it). The fact is, though, that
this point allows me to reverse the perspective of my
argument. The source of the 'incoherences' I have mentioned is usually traced to the 'intractability' of the nature
of international life. If this intractability really were to
blame, we would be forced to acknowledge, *in corpore vili*,
the homogeneity and consistency of each and every foreign policy. But this does not correspond to fact, as we
have seen. I tentatively deduce the hypothesis, therefore,
that the alleged danger and difficulty of international life
does not depend on nature, but on a deliberate choice
made by states. Setting abstraction aside, I now wish to
demonstrate that international life is not always uncontrollable after all. Let us consider the external political
conduct of states simply by viewing the effective policies
of great powers in the recent past. In their reciprocal
relations, the United States and the former Soviet Union
used to represent many other states; by deciding not to
consider themselves 'equal', the latter accepted, in return
for protection, a set of conditions definable in a word as
'representation'. In exchange for, or thanks to, this con-
cession, the two great representatives – the United States
and the former Soviet Union – were able, in practice, to
erase war from their reciprocal relations simply by coming
to terms on an end – the conservation of the status quo –
which might also be defined paradoxically as 'peace'. It is
of course impossible to arrive at results of such magnitude
at the stroke of a magic wand. The most effective means
of achieving them has proved to be that of permanent
bargaining, both with one's allies and with the opposite

party, both directly and explicitly, and through the tacit language of reciprocal deterrence.

It thus becomes clear that, if the type of relationship that bound the United States and the former Soviet Union were extended across the world, what would follow would be something as near as may be realistically imagined today to a peaceful international system. Insofar as it is the product of continuous negotiation, this might ultimately be an acceptable rough approximation of one form of international democracy. Its principal characteristic would be that neither party to the agreement would draw any advantage from breaking it. Yet it would be unfair for us to rest on our laurels and stop here: if it is possible to equalize peace and order, the same cannot be said of peace and democracy.[18] Although this argument allows us to reject the anarchic prejudice yet again, it still prevents us from transcending the conception of peace as a mere precondition for every future democracy. All of which risks turning my reasoning into a caricature of the ideal international democracy, a system in which each state would speak for itself and would have an equal right to be heard. On the other hand, I feel it has already emerged with some clarity that the main butt of my argument is the state, mainly in view of its niggardly international commitment – if it has any at all. If we observe the state solely and specifically from the domestic point of view, won't we discover that, in our age of so-called representation of interests, not even the votes of citizens are equal any more? How many other limits does democracy have in the countries lucky enough to possess it? A cursory glance at Amnesty International's periodic reports is a sufficient indicator of the dearth of democracy in the world today. It ought to be added, finally, that it is a specifically domestic shortcoming if governments enjoy great freedom of decision-making in the field of foreign policy. Yet, in view of the sometimes peremptory consequences of such decisions, there can be little doubt that this is one area in which more open consultation and control are in order.[19]

4   Democracy in the Future

My analysis of the last of the three aspects that I have identified in the problem of international democracy – the relationship between peace and democracy – has led not only to a complex, laborious explanation, but also to two conclusions that may appear contradictory. In reality, they are not. What has emerged is that, first of all, it is not sufficient for states to be democratic, each in its own right, for a democratic international regime to develop. But it is possible, secondly, for the conservation of peace to foster at least a 'pre-democratic' contractual procedure, although this depends to a large extent on states' observation of the rules of the game – in other words, on their sense of fair play. International life is not inherently evil; it becomes evil if a state wants it to. Hence, alongside the obvious and unquestionable conclusion that there is little or no democracy on the international stage today, it is still necessary to add that the present oligarchic situation in inter-state relations may develop forms of procedure involving an ever increasing number of states, and that this, in turn, could lead to the effective democratization of the international system. Furthermore, the lively theoretical debate which is raging among international relations scholars on the plausibility or otherwise of the hegemonic stability theory may also support my argument. The theory, which posits that the best arrangement for the international system is that in which one or more dominant states take decisions that are binding on all, allied and neutral states alike, cannot be verified in the contemporary world, simply because the level of international collaboration over the last forty years has proved to be inversely proportional to hegemonic stabilization.[20] On the one hand, it is argued that a hegemonized international system works well because, in it, one or two states decide for all the others and, the theory's most ardent supporters add, even unautonomous protected states gain nothing but benefits from such a situation. On the other, it is postulated that, far from irreparably damaging world peace, the progressive erosion of the Soviet–US duopoly's capacity to dominate any event on a planetary scale served to foster collaborative conduct internationally, and that such conduct increases as hegemonies decrease.[21] The question is: which is better, stabler and safer, a despotic international system or one which gives incentive to cooperation, hence democratization? Leaving exploration of the normative implications of the two positions to those directly concerned, criticisms of the hegemonic stability theory certainly strike home when they stress that, in any case, the decline of hegemonies has not worsened the standard of international life, but has if anything improved it by introducing intrinsically democratic stimuli for cooperation.

This conclusion is undeniably no less ingenuous and utopian than the one reached by the idealistic builders of the League of Nations. Democracies safeguard domestic regimes without extending them externally, yet when they act undemocratically externally, they also risk lowering the level of their own domestic democracy. If states have taken centuries to achieve an acceptable degree of democracy, how can we reasonably expect the international system – so young and so complex – to travel any faster? Isn't it perhaps true after all that a certain 'insensitiveness' to internationalism leads us to blame the nature of international life (*per se* much neglected) for the (all-'domestic') misdemeanours of certain states in their foreign policy? It was not international anarchy which induced the US government (or a part of it) to trade arms for souls (albeit of US citizens) with Iran, but rather questions of domestic – *democratic* – policy. For is not the conduct of someone selling arms to his worst enemy, who might then use the same arms against him, a conduct consonant with life in a condition of anarchy?

It seems to me, in other words, that the so-called ungovernability of the international system can be traced not to its alleged anarchy, but to the evident will of states to place domestic before international affairs. That this is the case may seem inevitable or necessary. But if we reflect that 'statehood' is *per se* a fact of international life, since no state exists without the existence of a plurality of analogous subjects, the domestic realm's pre-eminence over the external realm appears, logically speaking, totally unfounded, and, in any case, undemonstrable. If we add to this the consideration that any damage to a single state from the outside is, for reasons of scale, much greater than the damage that can be caused from the inside, then, even from the political point of view, the state of abandon in which the international dimension languishes (the potential source of total destruction) is all the more unacceptable.

Democratic culture has always regarded itself as progressive and its own diffusion as a benefit for humanity. Today international life may be in greater need of democracy than domestic life. I see no reason why we should not undertake to construct a normative theory of international democracy, and the first way of doing this is by arguing in favour of its feasibility.

5 Democracy and Justice

Does my agenda ultimately make domestic and international politics converge? I have located the roots of international democracy within states: does this mean that from now on they will concern themselves solely with their own affairs, thus inadvertently thwarting the positive effects of the diffusion of democracy? It may be argued that the opposite is true. If states no longer found their foreign policies on power,[22] they will be able to base their contacts with others no longer only on strategic and military evaluations, but also on political assessments, such as the approval or otherwise of their domestic political regimes. Wouldn't this, in turn, lead to a problem of democracy in inter-state relations? Once more, a truly original situation arises, and it is another element in favour of my thesis. The otherwise wide-ranging debate on international democracy over the last twenty years has concentrated solely and exclusively on the question of war. This has been the only yardstick for arguing or denying the innate peacefulness of democratic regimes as opposed to all others.[23] There has been no great concern with the (democratic) standards to which international relations might aspire in peacetime. Yet again, in an international situation in which the level of inter-state violence has decreased conspicuously, democratic theory must direct its interest not at the comparative war-proneness of democratic and authoritarian states, but at the capacity or otherwise of states to obey democratic rules in their reciprocal relations – in short, at the democratic standards of democratic states. The usual argument against this formulation may be summed up in the sceptical words of Norberto Bobbio: 'Is it possible for a state to be fully democratic in an (as yet) undemocratic world?'[24]

It is impossible to verify this condition fully, precisely because the society of states is not democratic. Yet, in my view, that is not the end of the story. Either we set out from the premise that nothing can be changed (in which case it would be hard to explain how states backed by despotic regimes have managed to become democratic), or we recognize that processes may be set into motion, and that, at a certain point, they turn into established facts, into tangible results. We can answer the first point by citing the international revolution of October 1989, which was in itself proof of the modifiability of that which is (or was). The second point reminds us of the transitional nature of a hypothesis such as that of the democratization of international politics.[25] The main doubt about the feasibility of this process (which Bobbio expresses) stems from the fact that there is currently no decision-making body to resolve conflicts peacefully. In the function it performs, the UN, for instance, is too pale a shadow of what it ought to be – namely, an unbiased third party.[26] One wonders, though, whether this formulation does not ultimately put the cart before the horse. Perhaps it is guilty of observing the process as if it were a fact without allowing it to exercise its admittedly slow, progressive influence.

If there is to be international democracy in the future, it will materialize in two distinct stages: first, at a domestic level within single countries and, second, in reciprocal relations between countries. I am not prepared to stick my neck out as to whether the two stages will take place in that order, although this is the sequence that has most commonly been imagined (from Kant onwards). The international community cannot influence domestic communities directly,[27] since any interference or pressure would obviously be regarded as a violation of the sovereignty of the recipient state. Although I believe a myriad of techniques might be used to foster this initial process indirectly, I am tempted to devote greater attention to the feasibility of the second (thus subverting the order of the factors). Hasn't the immense growth of forms of bargaining given rise to a sort of 'diplomatic democracy' over the last few decades? Haven't techniques of regime formation permitted the attenuation or resolution of once intractable disputes? And even when they fail to achieve specific results, such techniques manage, nonetheless, to keep the objects of controversy under cover.[28] It is thus possible to discover in the dynamics of international life today the procedural function which Bobbio has always recognized as playing a decisive role in the success of democracy (albeit only in formal and not substantial terms at first). Hence, the mounting recourse to accords, elaborated in continuous, reiterated international negotiations, might be considered as a token of the acceptance by states of the set of 'procedural rules' which presuppose 'a trend favourable to some of the values usually regarded as characteristic of the democratic ideal, such as the peaceful solution of social conflict, the elimination, where possible, of institutional violence, the frequent turnover of the political class, tolerance and so on.'[29] Another aspect to be considered, in parallel with that of diplomatic democracy, is the growing involvement of masses of electors in the elaboration of foreign policy decisions, especially through referendums. The latter are being resorted to with increasing frequency throughout the world, especially in Europe to decide Community-related issues.[30] It is of course hard to establish whether mass voting (which may undoubtedly be manipulated and which is invariably fired by strong passion) ensures more democratic outcomes than those generated by reserved cabinet decisions. Nonetheless, public discussion guarantees a degree of debate which is one of the great virtues of democracy, and which – in theory, at least – we have always recognized as fundamental.

Yet, the argument on the convergence of domestic and international democracy can be taken further still, if we pause to consider the potential influence on international life of the increase in number of democratic states. Many empirical studies have already shown not only that the democracy–pacifism nexus actually exists,[31] but also that the democratization process is the epidemiological product of an 'environmental effect'. More and more countries are recognizing the advantages of democracy over autocracy in the wake of the experience of their neighbours. The number of democratic states has increased not only in purely mathematical but also in regional terms.[32] In the period 1974 to 1987 (before the number of transitions to democracy increased still further), Europe showed a surplus (transitions towards democracy over transitions towards authoritarianism) of nine, Africa south of the Sahara a surplus of eight. Between 1984 and 1986, Latin America also showed a surplus of eight, and in the same period only the area of the Indian Ocean reported a deficit of five.[33] Yet these data would mean little if we failed to relate them to other considerations, such as the fact that not only do democratic states tend to be less war-prone, but that, when they do fight, they win. In the period 1816 to 1982, statistics reveal that democratic countries won 21 wars and lost only five.[34] This demonstrates that it is not true, as realist theory normally claims, that the nature of the domestic regime does not affect foreign policy, nor that democratic regimes work better than authoritarian ones. What it does demonstrate is that the diffusion of democracy is a powerful factor in combating war. Another empirical observation adds a further element: beaten states (mostly authoritarian, as we have seen) are very frequently subject to changes in regime,[35] which is tantamount to saying that the wars won by democratic states ultimately increase world democracy! In short, democratic states fight less than authoritarian ones but when they do, they win; and when they have won, democracy increases in the world (owing both to changes in regime and to their 'effect on the environment').

In view of such significant findings, we are forced to conclude with the value judgement that it is better for states to be democratic than authoritarian. The very history of democracy is the history of a process of continuous conquests, of civil and popular growth achieved over the centuries and culminating in the diverse forms of citizenship existing today. If democracy is a value,[36] shouldn't rulers feel duty-bound to acquire it, especially in view of its proven international qualities?[37]

Although this is admittedly nothing more than a regulatory idea, it is fair to ask whether states which are starting to act democratically in the presence of their peers are not bound to adopt suitably coherent forms of conduct domestically. On a number of occasions in the past, we saw the Soviet Union adopt more democratic conduct abroad than at home, while we saw the United States do the opposite. There would thus appear to be no firm nexus between the two cases. Yet it seems to me unlikely that a penchant for external democratic conduct can coexist with another for domestic anti-democratic conduct. This is another question which the idea of universal citizenship might solve. First, though, we must realize that an international democratic realm cannot exist as long as states fail to regard one another as equals, as entities among which the huge differences in power that caused rifts in the nuclear era have lost their *raison d'être*. On the contrary, it no longer seems rash for states to sit down together and discuss distributive (as well as remunerative) justice on a social and global plane.

Translated by John Irving

NOTES

1 Cf. R. Dahl, *Controlling Nuclear Weapons: Democracy Versus Guardianship* (Syracuse: Syracuse University Press, 1985); and R. Falk, 'Nuclear Weapons and the Renewal of Democracy', in A. Cohen and S. Lee (eds), *Nuclear Weapons and the Future of Humanity* (Totowa, NJ: Rowman & Allaheld, 1986).

2 Cf. B. Porter, 'Fabians, Imperialists and the International Order', in B. Pimlott (ed.), *Fabian Essays in Socialist Thought* (London: Heinemann, 1984). See also G. B. Shaw, *Peace Conference Hints* (London: Constable, 1919).

3 L. Woolf, *International Government* (London: Macmillan, 1916).

4 A. Zimmern, *The League of Nations and the Rule of Law* (London: Macmillan, 1936). On Zimmern, see D. J. Makwell, 'Sir Alfred Zimmern Revisited: Fifty Years On', *Review of International Studies*, 12: 2 (1986). On another extremely important figure in the cultural life of the time, G. Murray, cf. D. Wilson, *Gilbert Murray, 1866–1957* (Oxford: Clarendon Press, 1987). On the circumstances and cultural climate which allowed Zimmern to become the world's first professor of international relations, cf. E. L. Ellis, *The University College of Wales, Aberystwyth, 1872–1972* (Cardiff: University of Wales Press, 1972); and B. Porter (ed.), *The Aberystwyth Papers: International Politics 1919–1969* (Oxford: Oxford University Press, 1972).

5 A. Zimmern, 'Democracy and the Expert', *Political Quarterly*, 1: 1 (1930), p. 8.

6 R. Cecil, 'International Democracy', *Political Quarterly*, 5: 1 (1934), p. 329.

7 Ibid., pp. 339–40.

8 It is to the credit of its editors that the review welcomed 'opposition' articles such as the one by A. Salter, 'The Technique of Open Diplomacy', *Political Quarterly*, 3: 1 (1932), which stressed the difficulties encountered by 'open' diplomacy when it seeks to compensate for the undemocratic nature of secret foreign policy.

9 D. Thomson, 'International Democracy', *Political Quarterly*, 8: 1 (1937), p. 36.

10 The most recent reappraisal of the idealism–realism debate is that of M. Griffiths, *Realism, Idealism and International Politics* (London: Routledge, 1992).

11 E. H. Carr, *The Twenty Years' Crisis* (London: Macmillan, 1939).

12 L. Woolf, 'Utopia and Reality', *Political Quarterly*, 11: 2 (1940), p. 169.

13 One of the few research programmes oriented in this direction is G. Modelski's. See Modelski, 'The Long Cycle of Global Politics and the Nation State', *Comparative Studies in History and Society*, 20: 2 (1978); *Long Cycles in World Politics* (London: Macmillan, 1987); and Modelski (ed.), *Exploring Long Cycles* (London: Pinter, 1987).

14 M. W. Doyle, 'Kant, Liberal Legacies and Foreign Affairs', *Philosophy and Public Affairs*, 12: 3 (1982); N. Bobbio, 'Democracy and the International System', Chapter 1 in this volume.

15 Q. Wright, *A Study of War* (Chicago: University of Chicago Press, 1942), p. 841.

16 *The Federalist* (Chicago: *Encyclopedia Britannica*), n. 6, p. 40.

17 This is what is happening in the post-bipolar world, so far with disastrous results. But the fact that it is happening at all demonstrates at least that this way is practicable and that it may lead to improved outcomes in the future.

18 For there is of course no reason why an order should be innately democratic.

19 For an exploration of the statesman's moral responsibility in international politics, see M. I. Smith, 'Reasoning and Moral Responsibility in International Affairs', in K. N. Thompson (ed.), *Ethics and International Relations* (New Brunswick, NJ: Transaction Books, 1985). For a critical investigation with a philosophical slant, cf. R. Holmes, *On War and Morality* (Princeton: Princeton University Press, 1989), chs 2 and 3.

20 See D. Snidal, 'The Limits of Hegemonic Stability Theory', *International Organization*, 39 (1985), for proof of the fact. A totally different opinion is to be found in S. Strange, 'The Persistent Myth of Lost Hegemony', *International Organization*, 41: 4 (1987).

21 D. Snidal, 'The Limits of Hegemonic Stability', p. 580.

22 I use the reference to power as an abbreviation of those foreign policies which, nevertheless, concern themselves predominantly with defence of borders, and subsequently, if at all, with their expansion. As an example of the implications to which this type of policy leads, cf. F. E. Oppenheim, *The Place of Morality in Foreign Policy* (Lexington, MA: Lexington Books, 1991).

23 For a rich, updated bibliography, cf. the issue devoted to

the problem by the *Journal of Peace Research*, 29: 4 (1992). The debate is very lively at present: cf., at least, the exchange between A. Gilbert, 'Must Global Politics Constrain Democracy?' and S. D. Krasner, 'Realism, Imperialism and Democracy', both in *Political Theory*, 20: 1 (1992); and T. C. Morgan and V. L. Schwebach, 'Take Two Democracies and Call Me in the Morning: A Prescription for Peace?', *International Interaction*, 17: 4 (1992). Cf. also *International Interaction*, 18: 3 (1993), which is totally devoted to the topic.

24 N. Bobbio, 'Democracy and the International System', Chapter 1 in this volume.

25 I refer therefore to a process, not to a fact.

26 Cf. N. Bobbio, 'Democracy and the International System', p. 33

27 But I by no means rule out the importance of domestic democratic developments: for a quantitative survey, cf. S. P. Huntington, *The Third Wave: Democratization in the Late Twentieth Century* (Norman: University of Oklahoma Press, 1991).

28 The issue has inspired an impressive body of literature. For an overview, see L. Bonanate, A. Caffarena and R. Vellano, *Dopa l'anarchia* (Milan: Angeli, 1989). The development of the debate may be followed in *International Organization*, now tantamount to its official depository.

29 N. Bobbio, 'Democrazia', in N. Bobbio, N. Matteucci and G. Pasquino (eds), *Dizionario di politica* (Turin: Utet, 1976), p. 315.

30 Cf. both for a general formulation and for empirical data, J. T. Rourke, R. P. Hiskes and C. E. Zirakzadeh, *Direct Democracy and International Politics: Deciding International Issues Through Referendums* (Boulder, CO: Lynne Rienner, 1992).

31 See B. Russett, *Grasping the Democratic Peace* (Princeton: Princeton University Press, 1993). Russett is the author who, arguably, has explored international democracy more patiently and less polemically than any other.

32 According to the parameters adopted for some years now in the reports of R. Gastil (ed.), *Freedom in the World* (New York: Freedom House, 1989).

33 Cf. H. Starr, 'Democratic Dominoes: Diffusion Approaches to the Spread of Democracy in the International System', *Journal of Conflict Resolution*, 35: 2 (1991), p. 369.

34 Cf. D. A. Lake, 'Powerful Pacifists: Democratic States and War', *American Political Science Review*, 86: 1 (1992).

35 Cf. B. Bueno de Mesquita, R. M. Siverson and G. Woller, 'War and the Fate of Regimes: a Comparative Analysis', *American Political Science Review*, 86: 3 (1993).

36 This connotation explains why I include the 'democratization of the international system' among the five normative principles of international justice in *Ethics and International Politics* (Cambridge: Polity Press, forthcoming).

37 Not forgetting that democracy has sometimes failed to keep its promises, as N. Bobbio observes in *The Future of Democracy*. I do insist, though, that, internationally, its superiority over autocracy (violence, that is) still makes it the most preferable, if not the best imaginable, system (provided of course it keeps *this* 'promise' at least).

3

European Institutions, Nation-States and Nationalism

Mary Kaldor

The current period is characterized by integration and disintegration, fragmentation and interdependence, Europeanism and nationalism. Current political struggles are aimed not so much at control of existing forms of state power but at the construction of new forms of state power. Both Europeanism and nationalism have to be understood in this context.

The postwar period is often considered the apogee of the nation-state. It was only after 1945 that the entire globe was parcelled off into separate nation-states. Yet already, from the early twentieth century, the nation-state was becoming inadequate to cope with growing social, economic and military pressures in advanced industrial countries. In the early nineteenth century, proponents of the nation-state, such as Giuseppe Mazzini or Friedrich List, did not regard this as a final goal – an immutable creation. Rather, they had a functional view of the nation-state, as a viable political unit for democracy and industrialization. They saw it as a stage in human evolution, from local to national and eventually global society.

The early nationalists envisaged the construction and spread of a national language, for ease of communication, alongside local and regional dialects. It was only later when the nation was homogenized under the impact of a national language which was stabilized as a result of administrative support that the notion of the nation-state became tied to a notion of national culture and viewed not as a political artefact but as the natural political unit for a historically established national community. Mazzini, for example, did not support the independence of Ireland because he thought that Ireland was not viable as a nation-state.

In this essay, I suggest that the nation-state was and is a temporary phenomenon, even though there remains an extremely powerful attachment to the idea. The bloc system, which came into being as a result of the Cold War, can be viewed as a way of reconciling the attachment to the nation-state with the need for larger forms of political organization. However, the blocs were inherently contradictory forms of political organization and ultimately could not be sustained. Hence the current transition and the need to seek new approaches.

The basic argument is that to revert to nation-state forms of political organization in the post-bloc era would be anachronistic and hazardous. First, it would be a tragic error if the European Union became just another large nation-state, a European nation. The European Community was created, after World War II, on the basis of common agreement among West European nation-states, although its contains elements of supranationality. The challenge is how to enhance those elements of supranationality without constructing a new super nation. Secondly, modern nationalism, whether it is to be found in Eastern Europe or among the smaller nations of Western Europe, is not just a reversion to nineteenth-century nationalism. It is typically a twentieth-century phenomenon and it would be extremely dangerous if it were tied to nineteenth-century state forms.

In order to develop this argument, I try to establish a

framework for defining the characteristics of different forms of state power. The first two sections of the essay describe the characteristics of nations and blocs as forms of state power. The third section outlines some of the implications of post-industrialism or, rather, the current phase of industrialization for these characteristics. The last section sets out two models of future organization – a worst-case and a best-case model.

Characteristics of Nation-States

The nation-state is a particular form of the state. I share Giddens's view that many definitions of the state are actually definitions of the nation-state which is a state-form specific to the nineteenth and twentieth centuries.[1] What is meant by a state? In this essay, the state is defined as a dominant political organization. A political organization is an organization that exercises power, i.e. authority or control, over groups of human beings. A state is a political organization with a claim to sovereignty, i.e. a claim to be the dominant political organization within a particular realm, be it based on kinship, territory, or whatever.

The nation-state is a particular form of the state that came into being during the nineteenth century. It is extremely difficult to disentangle the concept of nation from the existence of a nation-state. Definitions of nation vary: a common linguistic group, inhabitants of particular territory, an ethnic group, a group with shared values or cultural traditions. In practice, a group of human beings that define themselves as a nation usually do so either because of the existence of a state, or because of their interest in establishing a state.

In what follows, I shall define four key characteristics of

state forms: political identity (i.e. the basis of sovereignty), culture, money and organized violence. Their forms for the nation-state are as follows:

(1) *Political identity* is based on *citizenship* which is linked to *territory*. This has a double aspect. First of all, *citizenship* implies some measure of assumed democratic control, even if many nation-states are in practice authoritarian and repressive; this is in contrast to *subjects*, which identify the relationship of individuals to dynastic regimes. Sovereignty is derived, at least in theory, from the citizen and does not reside with, say, the ruling monarch. Secondly, the citizen is the inhabitant of a particular *territory*. This is a contrast to, say, the Greek city-states, where citizenship was based on social stratification (i.e. the free citizen as opposed to the slave). Ethnically based concepts of citizenship are often contrasted with territorially based concepts of citizenship. In fact, a characteristic of the nation-state is that all concepts of citizenship are territorially based. Where citizenship is based on ethnic origin, as in Germany, the right to citizenship in a given territory is based on ethnicity. In other cases, e.g. France, all inhabitants of a particular territory have a right to citizenship, provided they acquire the national culture. The significance of ethnic concepts of citizenship is not that they are contrasted with territorially based concepts but that they link ethnicity and territory.

(2) *Culture* is vertical and homogenizing. In earlier societies, horizontal high cultures, generally independent of the state and linked to religion (e.g. Latin, Persian, Sanskrit, Mandarin Chinese), coexisted with a huge variety of vertical low cultures, based on vernacular language, customs, etc., and cultural diversity was an essential element of relatively stable social stratification.[2] The formation of the nation-state is associated with the spread of a national

written language, which gradually eliminates other languages, dialects and cultures.[3] Benedict Anderson talks about the emergence of an 'imagined community', made possible by the development of print technology. He sees the novel and the newspaper as key ingredients of imagined communities in which people who were not related by family ties, or who had never met, could feel themselves part of this common endeavour.[4] The rise of religious dissidence, which was also linked to the development of vernacular languages and the break-up of feudal ties of dependence associated with urbanization, also contributed to the decline of horizontal religious high cultures. The nation-state contributes to vernacularization and secularization through responsibility for cultural production (education).

This process of constructing an 'imagined community' took place organically in the West over a long period alongside the construction of new state forms. In contrast a national language, based on a dominant dialect, was often imposed savagely in the East – another factor which gives rise to ethnic and linguistic divisions. Another way of contrasting Western and Eastern concepts of citizenship derives from language. In the West, citizenship could be acquired through learning the national language, through assimilation (which could also be brutal). In the East, language was a birthright – it could not be acquired as a condition for citizenship later on.

(3) *Money* consists of a unified national currency issued by a *central bank*. Earlier, the minting of money was a royal prerogative, although, except in England from the Norman conquest onwards, a large number of kings, princes and noblemen had the right to create money. (In fifteenth-century Germany, there were six hundred coinage authorities.) The development of a centralized coinage and the control of money creation by central banks instead

of kings was an essential element in the rise of the nation-state.

The unification of currency was linked to regularization of banking, taxation and other administrative instruments associated with the rise of industrialization. A central discussion among theorists of the nation-state is about whether the nation-state was a product of industrialization. Gellner says that nations, not classes, were the outcome of industrialization. It would be excessively functionalist to argue that nation-states were established because of the requirements of industrialization. But one can say that earlier state forms were inadequate to cope with the demands of industrialization (for a mobile workforce able to communicate with one another, for infrastructure, administration and standard regulations, etc., all of which required a common language). And one can also argue that the nation-state succeeded, at least for a while, because it provided a viable framework for industrialization. In other words, there was a compatibility between political and economic developments.

(4) *Organized violence* takes the form of *national armies*, which represent its only legitimate form. Weber's definition of the state as 'a human community that (successfully) claims *the monopoly of the legitimate use of physical force* within a given territory'[5] actually applies only to the nation-state. In feudal states, for example, private armies existed and were tolerated by the state. The nation-state is characterized by the elimination of private armies, the decline of internal violence (e.g., violent forms of punishment, the use of physical violence in the exploitation of labour, etc.), the establishment of regular armed forces, together with all sorts of military innovations such as drill or professional staff, and the emergence of a distinction between the police (internal) and the military (external).

Tilly argues that the most important factor in the for-

mation of the nation-state was war.[6] Borders were established, ultimately, by war, not by language. The
requirements of war greatly expanded the administrative
reach of the state; in wartime, taxation was regularized
and extended, and after wars levels of public spending
never returned to prewar levels. And the need for taxes
and for soldiers required increased public consent to or
support for state activities.[7]

War both required and established the *legitimizing principle* of the nation-state. The legitimacy of the nation-state
derives from the fact that it is the only organization (it
possesses a monopoly of legitimate violence) that has
proved itself to be capable of defending borders. To this
can be added the notion that the inhabitants of a particular
territory share common national characteristics, a cultural
identity, that has to be defended against some 'other'.
Precisely because the nation-state is defined by borders,
the concept of nation is inherently *limited* and implies the
existence of other nations. Hence defence of, say, Britain
(i.e. British territory) can come to mean defence of British
culture (whatever that is) or ethnic Britons or the British
way of life.

The nation-state has had a short life by historical standards. It had many shortcomings which became increasingly evident in the twentieth century. It was too large to
protect cultures; cultural homogeneity involved the elimination of lesser cultures. Some were absorbed relatively
painlessly; others resisted and displayed separatist tendencies. It was also too large for efficient democratic
decision-making. Although the spread of the nation-state
was linked to self-determination and the establishment of
democratic institutions, nevertheless, the widening of the
suffrage, the tendency for majority rule, meant that real
participation in decision-making was very difficult and
that these democracies were very vulnerable to populism

– i.e., the appeal to irrational prejudices in order to win votes.

More importantly, the nation-state was too small to regulate what had become a global economy, especially after the introduction of mass production and mass consumption in the twentieth century. This task, undertaken by Britain in the nineteenth century, was no longer possible in the twentieth century. Likewise, the nation-state was too small to prevent wars, and this became critically important during the twentieth century when industrialization has so enormously increased the destructiveness of wars. The very fact that the legitimizing principle of nation-states was based on territory and nation meant that cooperation to regulate the economy or prevent wars was an *a priori* aberration.

Characteristics of Blocs

The basic elements of the bloc system came into being as a result of the alliances during World War II and were reproduced by the Cold War. The bloc system could be said to prefigure new post-nation state forms and at the same time to constitute a reversion to earlier state forms. The latter was especially true for the Soviet bloc, which retained some of the characteristics of the dynastic Tsarist empire; the Soviet bloc could perhaps be described as a suzerain states system, to use Martin Wight's term.[8]

The characteristics of the bloc system were as follows:

(1) *Political identity* is based on national *membership* of the bloc, which in turn is based on *ideology* (i.e. a commitment to parliamentary democracy and capitalism in the West or to socialism in the East). Unlike nationalism, which is inherently *limited*, blocism is, in principle, *universal* and limited only by the refusal of other states to accept the

ideology. Borders are not necessarily fixed and blocs can accept new members (e.g., Spain or Cuba.).

(2) The cohesion of the blocs is based on a common *horizontal culture* linking elites. Each bloc was characterized by an elite discourse which linked members of the bloc. In the West, this took the form, primarily, of arcane debates about strategy, especially nuclear strategy, through which political differences within blocs were articulated and mediated.[9] In the Soviet bloc, the language of Marxist-Leninism provided the medium for inter-party communication, which was what held the bloc together.

(3) For the Western bloc, the characteristic form of *money* was *hegemonic*. The need for international money became apparent at an early stage of industrialism. In the nineteenth century, sterling functioned as international money, alongside the gold and silver standards. The postwar monetary system was essentially a dollar system, although the dollar was not delinked from gold until 1971. This was linked to the various postwar institutions which underpinned the liberal world economy and the growth of international trade and investment. Although the Soviet bloc operated, in theory, on a rouble system, inter-bloc trade was, in practice, a kind of barter system in which roubles served as a standard of value; this was supplemented by world prices, but not as a means of exchange or a store of value. Direct integration of production, especially military production, was significant, however.

(4) *Armed forces* were organized in *integrated command structures*. This effectively meant the abandonment of national control over the means of organized violence, except in the case of the dominant powers, the United States and the Soviet Union. Apart from Britain and France, members of the blocs were not capable of waging

purely national wars; hence what had been viewed as an important element of sovereignty was abrogated.

The bloc system came into being as a result of the experience of World War II, which was fought, at least in rhetoric, not for territory but for principles – freedom and socialism. In both political and economic terms, the war appeared to resolve many prewar problems. The Cold War reproduced that experience. The *legitimizing principle* drew on the experience of defending ideas which had inspired millions of people. Since these ideas were universal, they justified, in principle, an unlimited use of force. The Cold War can be described as an 'imaginary war' which established the boundaries of a new imagined community based on ideas rather than territory or ethnos. The 'imaginary war' involved a permanent on-going confrontation in which, day after day, soldiers, military planners, spies, etc., engaged in continuous defence of the idea. The military confrontation became a *spectacle*, rather than a Clausewitzean instrument for the rational pursuit of geo-political objectives – i.e., the defence of borders or communications.

In what sense did the blocs prefigure new state forms? They were not simply new coalitions of nation-states. In the notion of an ideological community, rather than a territorially based or culturally based community, in the *a priori* if not *de facto* universalism of the bloc, in the construction of new horizontal elite cultures, in the creation, in theory, of international money and, above all, in the limitations on national armed forces, the bloc system marked a decisive break with the nation-state. On the other hand, the fact that the United States and the Soviet Union were dominant powers, the use of the dollar as international money and the ability of the United States and the Soviet Union to wage imperial wars were all characteristics of earlier epochs. In particular the blocs resembled nations in that, in practice, ideology tended to become identified with territory, much as cultural concepts of the nation had become identified with territory. Hence defence of freedom effectively meant defence of the West and defence of socialism effectively meant defence of the East.

The bloc system did succeed in overcoming *some* of the shortcomings of the nation-state system – those that arose from the fact that the nation-state was too small. In the West, the bloc system enabled an expansion of markets, especially mass consumption, and the spread of mass-production technology. In the East, industrialization on the Soviet model, for good or for ill, became possible. Furthermore, the bloc system suppressed (although not entirely) national wars and was able, through the concept of deterrence, to retain the idea of war as a legitimizing principle while avoiding the destructiveness of its actuality.

Precisely because the bloc system was transitional, a kind of half-way house between the nation-state and something else, it contained its own limitations. The elision of ideology with territory was fundamentally contradictory, and both the Western peace movement and the Eastern opposition were able to exploit this contradiction during the 1980s. The peace movement was able to point up the fundamentally undemocratic nature of nuclear weapons and the discourse of nuclear strategy; Solidarity and the movements which followed were able to claim, 'We are the people.'

The dominance of the United States and the Soviet Union also imparted an inflexibility to the system; they remained dominant even when they were no longer capable of genuinely representing the dominant idea, when the equation of the United States with democracy or the Soviet Union with socialism no longer resonated to the citizens of other members of the bloc. One of the advantages often touted for the nation-state in contrast to earlier empires is flexibility; hegemony can pass from one nation to another while the system remains intact. This was not the case with the bloc system.

The bloc system also shared some of the limitations of the nation-state – those that arise from the fact that the nation-state was too large and could not satisfy cultural or democratic aspirations. And it has also turned out to be inadequate to cope with the variety of demands for interdependence and flexibility that arise from the new phase of industrialization, sometimes known as post-industrialism or alternatively as the information age, which can be said to have developed during the last two decades.

The Current Phase of Industrialization

During the 1970s and 1980s, a revolution occurred in what is generally known as information technologies. This revolution is the consequence of the combination of large-scale data-processing, made possible by the use of micro-electronics, and enormous improvements in telecommun-ications, both because of the use of mico-electronics for switching and because of new forms of transmission, such as fibre optics and satellites. This revolution has had and is having a profound impact on all aspects of economic, social and political life – so much so that it is sometimes described as post-industrialism or at least an entirely new phase of industrialization comparable with the original industrial revolution.

In particular, the new technology does seem both to speed up global integration of economies and, at the same time, to make possible greater decentralization of both production and consumption. On the one hand, the ability of nation-states to influence national economies continues to be eroded by the globalization of production, trade and finance. On the other hand, mass production and mass consumption in a physical sense are less important. Instead of the production of standardized products on huge assembly lines, it is possible to produce reprogrammable standardized machines that can cater to a much wider variety of tastes and produce in much smaller quantities, so that products and production processes can be organized around local skills and local markets.

I do not wish to suggest that political institutions are determined by technology. The technology itself is a consequence of wider economic, social and political trends – the capitalist drive for ever-increasing productivity, the need to save space, energy and raw materials and to find new market niches, the particular form of skill stratification in Japan which first integrated these technologies into production processes, the military quest for accuracy, and so on. But it would be equally wrong to deny the impact of the new technology on political institutions. And, by the same token, political institutions will shape the future direction of technology. In what follows, I describe the interaction of technology and other developments on each of the characteristics of forms of state power.

(1) *Political identity*: Bloc identity, which had already been eroded over a long period, disappeared with the end of the Cold War, as did certain ideological identities (e.g., socialism). The reassertion of national identity is paradoxically combined with a weakening in the two elements of national identity – territoriality and citizenship. International trade and communication weaken the individual identification with territory. The written word is increasingly supplanted by television, film and international products – global cultural artefacts. Citizenship, moreover, tends to be confused with consumerism. Premodern methods of electioneering (public meetings, door-

to-door canvassing, pamphlets), which involved public involvement in debate, are more and more replaced by advertisements, party political broadcasts and televisual events designed around marketing techniques and based on opinion-poll data. The citizen chooses a candidate in much the same way as he or she chooses a product, and the candidate is packaged according to image consultants, etc. Increasingly, political parties, which used to be the site of political debate, are transformed into electoral machines. This development is particularly important in relation to parties of the left. The great political contribution of social democrat and communist parties was to involve the working classes in political debate, to provide a mechanism whereby ordinary people had access to the institution of the state. The political parties could be said to be the transmission belt between civil and political society, the way in which day-to-day concerns are translated into political demands. As parties of the left captured power and were integrated into political society, their grass-roots role diminished. The substitution of advertisement for public meetings, photo opportunities for hustings, etc., all exacerbate this tendency and result in a process of depoliticization. Democracy was always vulnerable to populism – the appeal by politicians to popular irrational prejudices. This vulnerability is enhanced both by the erosion of political culture – depoliticization, absence of political debate, rejection of dominant political ideas – and by the use of new techniques.

(2) *Culture*: Transnational communication, especially the use of telephones and faxes, makes possible all kinds of new horizontal networks, which are not necessarily elite networks. Corporations, universities, churches, trade unions – all are able to engage in much greater travel, exchange and international cooperation than formerly. In terms of political culture, it is possible to identify two

kinds of horizontal network which are relevant for future institution-building.

(a) The new nationalisms in Eastern Europe are actually transnational in character. It was always the case that national movements were able to call on the support of exiles. Today, that element in national movements is much more important for two reasons. One is the desire of large groups of expatriates in new nations, such as the United States, Canada or Australia, to reassert their cultural identities. (Perhaps this results from the longing to escape from the materialist cultural anonymity that characterizes these large new states.) The other is the ease of communication – the speed at which expatriate groups can provide money, ideas, arms, advice, techniques, etc. The role of Tyminski in Poland or of Canadian mercenaries in Croatia are examples of this kind of influence. The element of diaspora nationalism, associated with the need for a cultural homeland, is a very significant new phenomenon in re-emerging European nationalisms.

(b) One of the interesting features of the new social movements that emerged in the 1970s and 1980s is their transnational character. This is in contrast to earlier emancipatory movements, say the liberal and labour movements, which aimed at access to national politics. These movements arose partly because of the way in which the political parties have vacated the emancipatory part of the political spectrum on account of their preoccupation with state power. They have taken up the grass-roots role for at least some sectors of society. And yet because of the existence of parties of the left they have been rather unsuccessful at transforming themselves into political parties, and indeed they have often adopted an anti-party stance. However, in contrast to political parties, groups such as Amnesty International and Greenpeace have been very successful in developing transnational constituencies.

(3) *Money*: The typical feature of the current period is the absence of international monetary management either via a hegemon (e.g., the United States) or some new bloc or coordinated international institutions. Although hegemonic money still exists, enabling the United States to sustain a huge external trade deficit, the growth of international liquidity and the increase in the size and speed of capital flows greatly complicates national economic management, exacerbates international disequilibria, and prevents a solution to the twin problems of debts and deficits. Electronic technology – faxes, computers, plastic cards, etc. – have greatly speeded up financial transactions and exacerbated the speculative consequences of disequilibria and the inadequacies of national monetary control. Susan Strange talks about 'casino capitalism' to describe the current functioning of the international economy.[10]

(4) *Organized violence*: The character of war is changing dramatically. Nowadays, the case for NATO is based on the argument that it prevents the renationalization of armed forces. Through NATO, through various cooperation arrangements such as NACC, the North Atlantic Cooperation Council, and through various arms control arrangements, national armed forces are being integrated into loose transnational organizations. On the other hand, the break-up of multinational empires, rapid reductions in military spending and the withdrawal of Soviet troops from Eastern Europe are all factors which are leading to the re-emergence of private armies, through the sale of arms and mercenaries and the fragmentation of national armies. Hence the monopoly of organized violence is undermined both through transnationalization and privatization. How do these developments interact with technology? It has often been argued that the advent of nuclear weapons means that war can no longer be an

instrument of policy, since nuclear weapons cannot be used. The advent of information technologies, as well as other technologies, has greatly increased the accuracy and destructiveness of all munitions. The possibility of using force to achieve limited or defined objectives, at least against a similarly armed opponent, has diminished. On the other hand, it is not only the potential for destructiveness which has increased but also the distance between the destroyer and the destroyed. War is experienced both at home and by the operators of weapons as a television screen, making it difficult to distinguish between fiction and reality. If the possibilities for achieving geopolitical aims are declining, the opportunities for war as spectacle, as a symbolic legitimizing event, are widening. Hence there is a frightening gap between war as spectacle, as legitimation for new transnational arrangements, and the destructive reality of war fought by new private armies.

After the Blocs

Two possible models for the future can be outlined as set out in Table I. One is a combination of nations and bloc/nations (model A). The other is a new set of horizontal international state structures, prefigured by the blocs but not based on the imaginary war legitimizing principle, combined with vertical, territorially based, relatively small national units (model B). They are, in a sense, worst-case and best-case models, designed to help us think about future possibilities. Reality depends on how people act now. There are possible outcomes of the present situation, among many possible outcomes. What actually happens depends on political choices. These two models are described in order to help inform our political choices.

According to model A, the Western bloc re-creates itself either as separate US, Japanese and West European blocs or as a Western bloc with a cohesive 'European pillar'. The European Community remains primarily Western, possibly including some East European countries such as Hungary, Poland, the Czech Republic or maybe Slovenia. The key features of model A are the fact that the advanced industrial countries form a coalition based around a military alliance or a set of military treaties, and the integration of (Western) Europe involves the construction of a European nation-state with a European currency and a European army. The rest of Europe (and the Third World) reverts to nation-states, with emphasis on cultural or ethnic elements of national identity.

The characteristics of model A are:

(1) *Political identity*: This consists of citizenship/consumership, based on territoriality but with a strong ethnic or cultural component as far as Western Europe is concerned and based on ethnicity for the smaller nation-states. Already a notion of Europe as Christian (Catholic or Protestant but not Orthodox) and white is emerging. Slovenians and Croatians claim they are Europeans and Serbs are not. Similarly, citizenship of the smaller European nations is based on ethnicity. Those of Hungarian/ German/Polish, etc., origin can reclaim their citizenship, just as is the case for Jews *vis-à-vis* Israel. Antall, the Hungarian Prime Minister, said he was Prime Minister of all Hungarians, those living outside Hungary (in Serbia, Romania, Slovakia, Austria, the United States, etc.) as well as those living on the territory of Hungary. The implication is that he is not Prime Minister of those non-Hungarians (e.g. Jews and gypsies) living in Hungary.

(2) *Culture*: A unifying international materialist culture characterizes the European state, as in the case of the United States, combined with a notion of ethnic Europeanism. Cultural nationalism, both vertical and horizon-

Table 1 Two models of future European organization

	Cold War order		Model A		Model B	
	Nation-states	*Blocs*	*European nation-state*	*Nation-states*	*European institutions*	*Regional, local, units*
Political identity	Citizenship/territory	Membership/ideology	Citizenship/territory	Citizenship/ethnos	Membership/issue based	Citizenship/territory
Culture	Vertical and homogenizing national	Horizontal elite culture based on shared discourse	Vertical and horizontal homogenizing materialist	Vertical and horizontal homogenizing national	Horizontal green/peace, etc.	Diverse vertical and horizontal national/local cultures
Money	Unified bank money	Hegemonic money	Bloc currencies	National currencies linked to blocs	International money	International money, perhaps with separate national designs
Organized violence	National monopoly of organized violence	Integrated command structure; loss of national control of armed forces	European army	National armies	International security arrangements	Small national armies linked to international security arrangements; loss of national control of armed forces

tal, with strong homogenizing and exclusive tendencies characterizes those areas outside Europe.

(3) *Money*: Money takes the form of currency blocs: the dollar, the ECU and the yen, with smaller national currencies linked to one of the blocs.

(4) *Organized violence*: A European army is created as well as national armies.

In this model, the role of a European army becomes important as a form of legitimacy. The *raison d'être* of a European state is defence against the 'other' – the 'other' being non-European (orthodox, Muslim, black) and characterized by fundamentalism, chaos, violence, nationalism. The cohesion of the new state is based on a market principle, and democratic institutions are established relatively remote from individuals and localities, held together through opinion-poll democracy, the manipulation of citizen as a consumer. The role of the European army is to control borders and/or to intervene in external chaos. The Gulf War represented a kind of preview of this role. Although it was a real war, it was experienced in Europe and America as spectacle. The principle was democracy plus market economy versus fundamentalism. (The latter could include both religious fundamentalism and exclusive nationalism, as is emerging in Eastern Europe.)

Outside the European state, exclusive culturally based nationalism thrives, with growing populist authoritarianism and the spread of violence on the Yugoslav model. These nationalisms are horizontally linked to Europe and the West through migrant communities, and yet at the same time substantiate the concept of 'other'. They are both connected and opposite.

The characteristics of model B are:

(1) *Political identity*: The political identity of the new institutions consists of voluntary *membership* which is *issue based* rather than territorially based. That is to say, they are concerned with particular issues – human rights, security, the environment, economic and financial management. Their territorial reach varies and is open to addition through voluntary membership. Thus, membership of the CSCE covers the whole of Europe plus North America. The European Community might cover Western and Central Europe with a separate Commonwealth economic community of the former Soviet area. And so on. Small local and national units derive their *sovereignty* from citizens – i.e., the inhabitants of a particular territory base. These citizens have cultural links with expatriates but not military links.

(2) *Culture*: There is a horizontal political culture based on a commitment to solve certain shared global problems i.e., green/peace/development/human rights. This is combined with a multiplicity and diversity of local popular cultures based on a relatively small local and national territorial units.

(3) *Money*: National or bloc currencies are linked to a genuine form of international money guaranteed by international monetary institutions which are democratically accountable – i.e., a democratized IMF.

(4) *Organized violence*: National armed forces remain more or less as cultural relics (Scottish bagpipers, Croatians in Austro-Hungarian uniforms), but the national capacity to wage war is severely curtailed by a series of interlocking security arrangements, including multinational units and a complex mutual inspection framework arising from arms-control agreements, prefigured by the blocs.

There are general features of this model that should be mentioned. First of all, the horizontal institutions are different from what is known in international relations literature as an international regime. An international regime is a voluntary association of states who have come together to regulate some aspect of their relations. Sovereignty still rests with the nation-state and, by and large, the workings of those so-called regimes are mysterious, well beyond the public gaze. These new horizontal institutions do have a degree of sovereignty, that is to say, they can, in certain specified respects, interfere with the functioning of smaller units, be they nations, regions or municipalities. This was also the case with the blocs; however, their sovereignty derived from the dominance of the Soviet Union and the United States and the ideological coercion of 'imaginary war'.

If the new institutions are to be more than regimes and do not depend on some external threat for legitimacy, they require some functioning democratic principle. That means, first, that their field of competence has to be defined – respect for human rights, conflict resolution, international financial management – and limited. The principle of subsidiarity, as it is known in EC jargon, means that as many decisions as possible are taken by the smallest political units. This is essential for genuine democratic involvement. Second, these horizontal institutions have to be open and accountable to public opinion. How this is to be done has to be discussed and experimented with. There have to be formal rules for accountability – say, direct elections to an international parliament or an assembly of local territorial units. However, as is evident in the EC case, turn-out in elections is often low and these institutions seem remote from everyday concerns. More importantly, the process of governance has to change. Unlike centralizing nation-states, these new institutions have to have enabling mechanisms which essentially provide conditions (by means of funding, legal arrangements, even military protection) through which

local institutions, both governmental and non-governmental, can solve problems. In other words, democracy
would be about redistribution of power and participation
– an informal process underpinned by formal rules. If
current institutions are to develop in this way (and, to some
extent, the European Community already exhibits some of
the features I have described), then this must come about
organically and cannot be imposed from above by existing
states. This is why the development of a transnational
political culture that addresses the subjects, the fields of
competence of horizontal institutions, is so important.

The Helsinki Citizens Assembly, which is a coalition of
individuals and civic initiatives in East and West, is a
deliberate attempt to create a new horizontal non-governmental structure which can engage with international
institutions. A key feature of the political thinking of the
new movements is the commitment to affect ideas as a
way of influencing power rather than capturing power.
The argument is that honest debate is very difficult in
party politics because electoral considerations influence
expressed opinion. In the era of opinion polls and advertisements this problem is all the more serious. Havel's
concept of anti-politics or 'Living with Truth' was an
attempt to introduce serious, honest debate into politics.
This notion of a transnational debating forum, designed
to widen the scope of debates about public affairs, is
absolutely necessary if democracy is to be deepened both
at an international and a local level and if we are to move
away both from war as war and war as spectacle.

Secondly, the smaller units in model B can be national,
regional or municipal. National units continue to exist but
they are no longer nation-states. They have lost the
characteristics of nation-states because, even though
they are territorially based, they have to share sovereignty
with both smaller and larger units. They may continue
to possess armed forces but the ability to wage war

independently is abrogated. They may continue to possess separate currencies but money creation is limited by membership in regional and international financial organizations. They continue to protect and propagate national culture and language but they cannot exclude other cultures.

Essentially, the national units could be viewed as repositories of culture – using the term culture in the broad sense to include types of education, the preservation of language(s), the pattern of ownership, the type of health-care provisions, etc., determined by local demands and restrained only by common international standards concerning human rights (including economic and social rights and the rights of the minorities), environmental protection, security and so on as guaranteed by the horizontal organizations. There is no reason, in fact, why the national units should not also extend horizontally, so that expatriate communities could have formal links with a 'cultural homeland' and so that different national units overlap and extend over the same territories. Some kind of mechanism that would allow individuals to choose identity or even to possess multiple identities could be invented, with overlapping citizenships. The aim would be to preserve and encourage multicultural diversity. Moreover, this role need not be confined to national units. Regional and local differences could also be protected and celebrated through an enhanced role for municipalities and regional governments.

Tendencies for both models can be observed in the current turbulent period. The role of the European Community in the Yugoslav crisis is instructive in terms of the evolution of new political institutions in Europe. The Yugoslav war exhibits all the contradictory elements of the current phase. It cannot be described as a classic inter-nation-state war on the Clausewitzean model. But nor can it be described as a civil war. On the one hand, it is fought by private armies and is about the fragmentation of territory. On the other hand, there is a pervasive transnational involvement, including humanitarian organizations, diaspora nationalists, peace-keeping troops, etc.

It is very difficult to envisage any classic nation-state-based solution, however many political units are eventually established in the area that used to be Yugoslavia. Peace and stability could be restored only if these units have certain clear limitations on sovereignty not only in the field of human and minority rights but also on economy and security. The elections which brought to power nationalist populist politicians were classic examples of the degeneration of politics resulting from the absence of political culture and the use of new techniques. There is no possible solution based on compromise between these politicians; even if they can agree on the carve-up of territory, the outcome would be small closed-in authoritarian states which would be unviable in the long term. Any effort to find a solution has to focus on mechanisms for genuine civic participation in debates about the future of the region. The role of new transnational institutions has to be an enabling one, establishing a framework, even to the extent of providing military force, in which a democratic process free of fear can be established. This is the purpose of proposals for international protectorates.

In so far as the European Community tried to mediate the conflict, sending humanitarian aid and multinational peace-keeping troops, it did begin to act as a new type of horizontal institution, foreshadowing the possibility of a civil Europe with a political and not a military conception of its role. However, the approach of the European Community was also West-centric and state-centric. Yugoslavia, in West European newspapers, is said to be a crisis at 'Europe's gates' or on 'Europe's doorstep', not in

Europe. Policy options were the result of internal compromises among the EC states rather than the result of the actual situation in Yugoslavia. They could only envisage a solution based on nation-states, and the choice they opted for – a unitary state or a collection of new ethnically based states – depended on their own internal biases. Initially, the European Community took a pro-federation position which seemed to legitimize the role of the Yugoslav army in Slovenia and Croatia. Then, under German pressure, the European mediators concentrated exclusively on politicians, indicating their inter-governmental myopia and their scepticism about the role of citizens; they were rather unwilling to meet with and make more visible peace groups in the different republics who could put pressure on nationalist politicians.

Possible solutions were increasingly presented in terms of two unacceptable alternatives. One was to say that all sides are responsible and that, if no compromise can be reached, then no solution is possible. This is a Balkan civil war from which it is best to keep out. The other was to take the side of Croatia, Slovenia and later Bosnia and to argue for full-scale military intervention. The alternatives for local protectorates in which the international community would provide space for democratic processes were largely ignored.

In other words, the Yugoslav crisis anticipates the possibility of both approaches. In the mediation approach of both the European Community and the United Nations, and in the role of transnational peace networks, it is possible to envisage the emergence of horizontal state structures which are not legitimized in terms of military protection against an external threat. On the other hand, because of its Western nature and its state approach, the European Community was gradually pulled into a mixture of *laissez-faire* and one-sidedness which could foreshadow a new West–East division of Yugoslavia and of Europe,

banishing Serbia and Bosnia as well to the nether world
of violence and chaos 'outside Europe'.

The choice between model A and model B depends on
two factors. First, it requires that the construction of the
post-Cold War order is regarded as a common endeavour
and not just a Western endeavour. Eastern Europe and,
indeed, the Third World have to be brought into the
international system. This involves responsibilities on
both sides. An overly West-centric view of the world
which excludes Eastern Europe and the Third World will
exacerbate (it already has) exclusivist violent tendencies
within those countries. By the same token, exclusivist
violent tendencies in Eastern Europe and the Third World
will provide an argument for exclusion. Western blocism
will feed on nationalism and religious fundamentalism
and vice versa, just as NATO fed on Soviet totalitarianism
and vice versa. So far, the tendencies are not hopeful.
Although East European countries are allowed to join the
IMF, the OECD and the World Bank, and there is talk of
associate membership of the European Community when
they are rich enough, which may take a long time, the
CSCE is still very weak in comparison with NATO, and
the readiness to solve the vast common environmental
and economic problems has not been as great as it might
have been.

Secondly, model B requires a change of thinking and
the construction of a political culture around that change
of thinking. So long as people stick to nation-state conceptions, model A is much more likely.

An alternative way of thinking that seeks a consensual
approach to international institutions can arise only out of
the existence of a transnational political culture that can
create a transnational public opinion. To some extent this
does already exist through the horizontal networks created by green/peace/human rights groups.

NOTES

1   See Anthony Giddens, *A Contemporary Critique of Historical Materialism*, Vol. 2: *The Nation-State and Violence* (Cambridge: Polity Press, 1985).
2   See Ernest Gellner, *Nations and Nationalism* (Oxford: Blackwell, 1983).
3   At the time of the French Revolution only 50 per cent of the inhabitants of France spoke French, and at the time of Italian unification only about 2.5 per cent of Italians spoke Italian. According to Massimo d'Azeglio: 'We have made Italy, now we have to make Italians'; see Eric Hobsbawm, *Nations and Nationalism since 1870: Programme, Myth, Reality* (Cambridge: Cambridge University Press, 1990).
4   Benedict Anderson, *Imagined Communities* (London: Verso, 1991).
5   Max Weber, 'Politics as Vocation', in *Essays in Sociology* [1948] (London: Routledge, 1991), p. 78.
6   Charles Tilly, 'Reflections on the History of European State-making', in Tilly (ed.), *The Formation of Nation States in Western Europe* (Princeton: Princeton University Press, 1975).
7   Tilly says: 'Recurrently, we find a chain of causation running from 1) change or expansion in land armies to 2) new efforts to extract resources from subject populations to 3) the development of new bureaucracies and administrative innovation to 4) resistance from the subject population to 5) renewed coercion to 6) durable increases in the bulk or extractiveness of the state.' Ibid., p. 75.
8   See Martin Wight, *Systems of States* (Leicester: Leicester University Press, 1977).
9   See Chapter 10, 'Imagined Strategies', in Mary Kaldor, *The Imaginary War* (Oxford: Blackwell, 1990).
10   Susan Strange, *Casino Capitalism* (Oxford: Blackwell, 1989).

4

Democracy and the New International Order

David Held

Introduction

The international community is at a crossroads. The post-Cold War era ushered in the possibility of a 'new international order' based on the extension of democracy across the globe, and a new spirit of cooperation and peace. The enthusiasm with which this possibility was greeted seems now far removed. The crises in Bosnia, Somalia, Iraq, Cambodia and elsewhere have brought many to the conclusion that the new world order is a new world disorder. Many UN initiatives in conflict management and resolution – initiatives which have all too often been contested, reactive and underfunded – face stagnation or defeat. What are the causes of this disarray and fragmentation?

The argument which follows suggests that these causes can be traced to the contemporary form of democracy and the nation-state system itself. The chapter begins by asking how right we are to cheer for democracy. After examining some of the key interconnections which exist among states and societies, the chapter goes on to offer a new agenda for democratic thought and practice. While we cannot do without democracy, it is increasingly bankrupt in its traditional shape and, thus, needs fundamental reform, in the short and long terms. Addressing the changing international order, the case is made for 'a cosmopolitan international democracy'. The case for such a democracy is fraught with difficulties, but strong grounds are presented for its indispensability to the maintenance and development of democracy both within pre-established borders and across them.

The Celebration of Democracy?

Although the ideal of the active citizen, central to classical Athenian democracy, has met with suspicion and distrust for the best part of two and a half thousand years, we all champion democracy today: nearly everyone professes to be a democrat. The revolutions which swept across Central and Eastern Europe at the end of 1989 and the beginning of 1990 stimulated an atmosphere of celebration. Some recent political commentators have even proclaimed the 'end of history' – the triumph of democracy over all alternative forms of governance. Thus, for the much quoted Francis Fukuyama, contemporary democracy is the final and good political order because of all available political systems it alone stands as 'a reciprocal and equal agreement among citizens' to recognize each other.[1]

The classical conception of democracy placed the 'active citizen' at its centre. If political thinkers today proclaim the virtues of democracy, they are the virtues of a very different version of democratic life: liberal representative democracy. In the nineteenth and twentieth centuries, democracy gradually took on its distinctively contemporary form: a cluster of rules, procedures and institutions permitting the broadest involvement of the majority of citizens, not in political affairs as such, but in the selection of *representatives* who alone can make political decisions.

This cluster includes elected government; free and fair elections; universal suffrage; freedom of conscience, information and expression; the right of all adults to oppose their government and stand for office; and the right to form independent associations.[2] The consolidation of representative democracy, thus understood, has been ultimately a twentieth-century phenomenon – the result largely of sustained struggles by working-class, feminist and civil-rights activists. Perhaps one should even say that the consolidation of representative democracy has been a late twentieth-century phenomenon. For it is only in the closing decades of this century that democracy has been (relatively) securely established in the West and widely adopted in principle as a suitable model of government beyond the West.

The tale of democracy, therefore, seems to have a happy ending. Citizen-voters are, in principle, able to hold public decision-makers to account; while the decision-makers themselves represent the interests of their constituents – ultimately, 'the people' in a delimited territory. However, the tale cannot end here. Democracy has another dimension. In fact, it has several other dimensions. For example, there are complex issues involving the internal character of representative democracy. These relate to the connections between the spheres of the public and the private – between the possibility of citizenship and participation in a political community, and obstacles to such a possibility anchored heavily in unequal gender relations. And they relate to the connections between public authority and economic power – between the possibility of social and economic development and the substantial structural constraints on political action. These are all substantial matters which I, among many others of course, have addressed.[3] But they are *not* matters I wish to focus on directly here. The 'other dimension' of democracy I want to examine concerns the way the resolutions of the key questions of democratic theory and practice are challenged by the forces and processes of regional[4] and global inter-connectedness. At a time when the idea of 'the rule of the people' is more popular than ever, the very efficacy of democracy as a national form of political organization is open to doubt.[5]

National Communities in a Global Context

The problem is that national communities by no means make and determine decisions and policies exclusively for themselves, and governments by no means determine what is right or appropriate exclusively for their own citizens.[6] To take some topical examples: a decision to increase interest rates in an attempt to stem inflation or exchange-rate instability is most often taken as a 'national' decision, although it may well stimulate economic changes in other countries. A decision to permit the 'harvesting' of the rainforests may contribute to ecological damage far beyond the borders which formally limit the responsibility of a given set of political decision-makers. A decision to build a nuclear plant near the frontiers of a neighbouring country is a decision likely to be taken without consulting those in the nearby country (or countries), despite the many risks and ramifications for them. A decision by a government to save resources by suspending food aid to a nation may stimulate the sudden escalation of food prices in that nation and contribute directly to an outbreak of famine among the urban and rural poor. These decisions, along with policies on issues as diverse as investment, arms procurement and AIDS, are typically regarded as falling within the legitimate domain of authority of a sovereign nation-state. But, in a world of regional and global interconnectedness, there are major questions to be put about the coherence, viability and accountability of national decision-making entities themselves.

Further, decisions made today by quasi-regional or quasi-supranational organizations such as the European Community, the North Atlantic Treaty Organization, or the International Monetary Fund diminish the range of decisions open to given national 'majorities'. The idea of a community which rightly governs itself and determines its own future – an idea at the very heart of the democratic polity – is, accordingly, deeply problematic.

Developments putting pressure on democratic polities are often referred to as part of a process of 'globalization' – or, more accurately put, of 'Western globalization'. Globalization in this context implies at the least two distinct phenomena. First, it suggests that the chains of political, economic and social activity are becoming worldwide in scope. And, second, it suggests that there has been an intensification of levels of interaction and interconnectedness within and between states and societies. What is new about the modern global system is the spread of globalization in and through new dimensions of activity – technological, organizational, administrative and legal, among others – and the chronic intensification of patterns of interconnectedness mediated by the modern communications industry and new information technology. Distant localities are now interlinked as never before. Globalization has reordered both time and space and has 'shrunk the globe'.[7]

It could be objected that there is nothing particularly new about global interconnections, and that the significance of globalization for politics has, in principle, been evident for some time. Such an objection could be elaborated by emphasizing that a dense pattern of global interconnections began to emerge with the initial expansion of the world economy and the rise of the modern state from the late sixteenth century. Further, it could be suggested

that domestic and international politics have been inter-
woven throughout the modern era: domestic politics has
always to be understood against the background of international politics; and the former is often the source of the
latter.

However, it is one thing to claim that there are elements
of continuity in the formation and structure of modern
states, economies and societies, quite another to claim
that there is nothing new about aspects of their form and
dynamics. For there is a fundamental difference between,
on the one hand, the development of particular trade
routes, and the global reach of nineteenth-century
empires, and, on the other hand, an international order
involving the conjuncture of a global system of production
and exchange which is beyond the control of any single
nation-state (even of the most powerful); extensive networks of transnational interaction and communication
which transcend national societies and evade most forms
of national regulation; the power and activities of a vast
array of international regimes and organizations, many of
which reduce the scope for action of even leading states;
and the internationalization of security structures which
limit the scope for the independent use of military force
by states. While in the eighteenth and nineteenth centuries trade routes and empires linked distant populations
together through quite simple networks of interaction, the
contemporary global order is defined by multiple systems
of transaction and coordination which link people, communities and societies in highly complex ways and which,
given the nature of modern communications, virtually
annihilate territorial boundaries as barriers to socio-economic activity and relations, and create new political
uncertainties.

A Crisis of Legitimacy?

These developments place questions on the political
agenda which go to the core of the categories of modern
democratic thought. The idea that *consent* legitimates
government and the state system more generally has been
central to nineteenth- and twentieth-century liberal democrats. These democrats have focused on the ballot box as
the mechanism whereby the individual citizen expresses
political preferences, and citizens as a whole periodically
confer authority on government to enact the law and
regulate economic and social life. The principle of
'majority rule', or the principle that decisions which
accrue the largest number of votes should prevail, is at
the root of the claim of political decisions to be regarded
as worthy or legitimate. But the very idea of consent
through elections, and the particular notion that the
relevant constituencies of voluntary agreement are the
communities of a bounded territory or a state, become
open to question as soon as the issue of national, regional
and global interconnectedness is considered and the
nature of a so-called 'relevant community' is contested.

Whose consent is necessary and whose participation is
justified in decisions concerning, for example, AIDS, or
acid rain, or the use of non-renewable resources, or the
management of economic flows? What is the relevant
constituency: national, regional or international? To
whom do decision-makers have to justify their decisions?
To whom should they be accountable?

Territorial boundaries demarcate the basis on which
individuals are included and excluded from participation
in decisions affecting their lives (however limited the
participation might be), but the outcomes of these
decisions most often 'stretch' beyond national frontiers.
The implications of this are profound, not only for the

categories of consent and legitimacy, but for all the key ideas of democracy: the nature of a constituency, the meaning of representation, the proper form and scope of political participation, and the relevance of the democratic nation-state as the guarantor of the rights, duties and welfare of subjects. It was, after all, decisions of the European Court of Justice which led to changes in British law in the 1980s on issues as far ranging as sexual discrimination and equal pay.

Considerations such as these would probably come as little surprise to those nations and countries whose political independence and identity have been deeply affected by the hegemonic reach of empires, old and new, but they do come as a surprise to many in the West. However, these reflections ought in principle to cause little astonishment; for they go to the heart or 'deep structure' of the modern system of nation-states, which has been characterized by a number of striking features, including democracy *in* nation-states and non-democratic relations *among* states; the entrenchment of accountability and democratic legitimacy *inside* state boundaries and the pursuit of power politics (or maximum advantage) *outside* such boundaries; and democracy and citizenship rights for '*insiders*' and their frequent negation for '*outsiders*'.

The Westphalian Model of World Order

The conception of international order which emerged to clarify and formalize the inter-state system can be referred to as the 'Westphalian' model of sovereign power (after the Peace of Westphalia of 1648, which brought to an end the German phase of the Thirty Years' War).[8] The model covers a wide period from 1648 to 1945 (although some would argue it still holds today). It depicts the development of a world community consisting of sovereign states which settle their differences privately and often by force; which engage in diplomatic relations but otherwise demonstrate minimal cooperation; which seek to place their own national interest above all others; and which accept the logic of the principle of effectiveness, that is, the principle that might eventually makes right in the international world – appropriation becomes legitimation.[9]

The upshot of this framework of international affairs is that states have rarely been 'subject to international moral requirements because they represent separate and discrete political orders with no common authority among them.'[10] In this situation, the world consists of separate political powers, pursuing their own interests, backed ultimately by their organization of coercive power. Moreover, the resort to coercion or armed force by non-state actors contesting territorial boundaries is also, arguably, an almost inevitable outcome. For communities contesting established territorial boundaries have 'little alternative but to resort to arms in order to establish "effective control" over the area they seek as their territory, and in that way make their case for international recognition (cf. Eritrea, East Timor, Kurdistan . . .).'[11]

The UN Charter Framework

Did the adoption of the UN Charter, after World War II, represent a break with the Westphalian logic of international governance? The Charter system was distinctively innovative in a number of ways; it provided a forum in which all the states were in certain respects equal, and a framework for unshackling many of the territories of former empires: decolonization. However, it would be misleading to conclude that the era of the UN Charter simply displaced the Westphalian conception of international regulation; for the Charter framework constitutes, in many senses, an extension of the inter-state system.

The organizations and procedures of the UN were designed partly to overcome weaknesses in the League of Nations. Its 'architecture', therefore, was drawn up to accommodate the international power structure as it was understood in 1945. The division of the globe into powerful nation-states, with distinctive sets of geo-political interests, was built into the Charter conception. As a result, the UN was virtually immobilized, in a manner that was particularly clear during the Cold War, as an autonomous actor on many pressing issues.[12]

One of the most obvious manifestations of this was the special veto power accorded to the five permanent members of the UN Security Council. Moreover, the Charter gave renewed credence (through Article 51) to unilateral strategic state initiatives if they were necessary in 'self-defence', since there was no clear delimitation of the meaning of this phrase. In addition, while the Charter placed new obligations on states to settle disputes peacefully, and laid down certain procedures for passing judgement on alleged acts of self-defence, these procedures have rarely been used. Even the UN's peace-keeping missions have been restricted (a key exception being Somalia) to areas in which the consent of the territorial state in question has first been given, sometimes with catastrophic consequences – as in, for instance, the territories of the former Yugoslavia. In sum, the UN Charter model, despite its many good aims, failed effectively to generate a new principle of organization in the international order – a principle which might break fundamentally with the logic of Westphalia and generate new democratic mechanisms of political coordination and change.[13]

Rethinking Democracy and the International
Order: the Cosmopolitan Model

How, then, should democracy be understood in a world
of independent and interconnected political authorities?
In my view, the problem of democracy in our times is to
specify how democracy can be secured in a series of
interconnected power and authority centres. For democracy involves not only the implementation of a cluster of
civil, political and social rights (freedom of speech, press
and assembly, the right to vote in a free and fair election,
a universal and free education, and so on), but also the
pursuit and enactment of these rights in intergovernmental and transnational power structures. Democracy can
only be fully sustained in and through the agencies and
organizations which form an element of and yet cut across
the territorial boundaries of the nation-state. The possibility of democracy today must, in short, be linked to an
expanding framework of democratic states and agencies.[14]
I refer to such a framework as 'the cosmopolitan model of
democracy', by which I mean a system of governance
which arises from and is adapted to the diverse conditions
and interconnections of different peoples and nations.
How should it be understood?

To begin with, the cosmopolitan model of democracy
requires, as a transitional measure, that the UN system
actually lives up to its Charter. Among other things, this
would involve pursuing measures to implement key elements of the rights conventions, enforcing the prohibition
on the discretionary right to use force, and activating the
collective security system envisaged in the Charter itself.
In addition, if the Charter model were extended – for
example, by adding the requirement of compulsory jurisdiction in the case of disputes falling under the UN rubric,
or by providing means of redress in the case of human

rights violations through a new international human rights court, or by making a (near) consensus vote in the General Assembly a legitimate source of international law (and recognized as such by the World Court), or by modifying the veto arrangement in the Security Council and rethinking representation on it to allow for adequate regional accountability – a basis might be established for the UN Charter system to generate political resources of its own, and to act as an autonomous decision-making centre. Thus, the UN could take a vital step towards shaking off the burden of the much-heard accusation that it operates 'double standards', functioning typically on behalf of the North and West – for instance, when it insists on military intervention to protect the sovereignty and legal autonomy of Kuwait because oil and energy policy are at stake, but leaves Bosnia to disintegrate; or when it fails to enforce UN resolutions against Israel while downplaying the case of the Palestinians. If the UN gained the means whereby it could begin to shake off this heritage, an important step could also be taken towards establishing and maintaining the 'rule of law' and its impartial administration in international affairs.[15]

While each move in this direction would be significant, particularly in enhancing the prospects of a global peace, it would still represent, at best, a movement towards a very partial or incomplete form of democracy in international life. Certainly, each state would enjoy formal equality in the UN system, and regional interests would be better represented. But the dynamics and logic of the inter-state system would still represent an immensely powerful force in global affairs; the massive disparities of power and asymmetries of resource in the global political economy would be left virtually unaddressed; *ad hoc* responses to pressing international and transnational issues would remain typical; there would be no forum for the pursuit of global questions directly accountable to the subjects and agencies of civil societies; and the whole question of the accountability of international organizations and global bodies would remain unresolved.

Thus, hand in hand with the changes already described, the cosmopolitan model of democracy would seek the creation of regional parliaments (for example, in Latin America and Africa) and the enhancement of the role of such bodies where they already exist (the European Parliament) in order that their decisions become recognized, in principle, as legitimate independent sources of law. The model anticipates, in addition, the possibility of general referenda of groups cutting across nations and nation-states on issues as diverse as energy policy, the balance between public and private transportation and the organization of regional authorities, with constituencies defined according to the nature and scope of controversial trans-national issues.

Furthermore, alongside these developments the cosmopolitan model of democracy would seek the entrenchment of a cluster of rights, including civil, political, economic and social rights, in order to provide shape and limits to democratic decision-making.[16] This requires that they be enshrined with the constitutions of parliaments and assemblies (at the national and international level); and that the influence of international courts is extended so that groups and individuals have an effective means of suing political authorities for the enactment and enforcement of key rights, both within and beyond political associations.

In the final analysis, the formation of an authoritative assembly of all democratic states and agencies – a reformed General Assembly of the United Nations, or a complement to it – would be an objective. Agreement on the terms of reference of an international democratic assembly would be difficult, to say the least. Among the difficulties to be faced would be the rules determining the

Assembly's representative base. One country, one vote? Representatives allocated according to population size? Could major international functional organizations be represented? But if its operating rules could be agreed – in an international constitutional convention, for example – the new Assembly would become an authoritative international centre for the consideration and examination of pressing global issues, for example, health and disease, food supply and distribution, the debt burden of the Third World, the instability of the hundreds of billions of dollars that circulate the globe daily, ozone depletion and the reduction of the risks of nuclear war.

Possible Objections

Of course, the idea of a new democratic international assembly is open to a battery of objections commonly put to similar schemes. Would it have any teeth to implement decisions? How would democratic international law be enforced? Would there be a centralized police and military force? And so forth. These concerns are significant. But many of them can be met and countered. For instance, it needs to be stressed that any global legislative institution should be conceived above all as a 'framework-setting' institution. Although a distinction ought to be made between legal instruments which would have the status of law independently of any further negotiation or action on the part of a region or state or local government, and instruments which would require further discussion with them, implementation of a broad range of recommendations would be a matter for non-global levels of governance. In addition, the question of law-enforcement at a regional and global level is not beyond resolution in principle; a proportion of a nation-state's military (perhaps a growing proportion over time) could be 'seconded' to the new international authorities and placed at their disposal on a routine basis. Or, better still, these authorities could increase enforcement capabilities by creating a permanent independent force recruited directly from among individuals who volunteer from all countries.[17] To this end, avenues could be established to meet the concern that 'covenants, without the sword, are but words' (Hobbes).

Equally, only to the extent that the new forms of military arrangement are locked into an international democratic framework would there be good grounds for thinking that a new settlement could be created between coercive power and accountability. If such a settlement sounds like a 'pipe dream', it should be emphasized that it is a pipe dream to imagine that one can advocate democracy today without engaging with the range of issues elaborated here. If the new emerging international order is to be democratic, these issues have to be confronted (even if their details are open to further specification and debate). Moreover, it needs to be stressed that to confront these issues is not to claim that a cosmopolitan model of democracy is immediately realizable – of course not! But who imagined the peaceful unification of Germany just a few years ago? Who anticipated the fall of the Berlin Wall and the retreat of communism across Central and Eastern Europe? The political space for a cosmopolitan model of democracy has to be made, and it is not inconceivable that some space will be made – for elements of it at least – in the wake of, for instance, a severe crisis of the global financial system, or of the environment, or of war. Political change can take place at an extraordinary speed, itself no doubt partially a result of the process of globalization.

Cosmopolitan Objectives: Short and Long Term

The cosmopolitan model of democracy presents a programme of possible transformations with short- and long-
term political implications. It does not present an all-or-
nothing choice, but rather lays down a direction of possible change with clear points of orientation. These include:

Short-term	Long-term
1 Reform of UN Security Council (to give the Third World a significant voice and to alter the veto system)	Global parliament (with limited revenue-raising capacity) connected to regions, nations and localities
2 Creation of a UN second chamber (perhaps on the model of the European Parliament)	New Charter of Rights and Duties locked into different domains of political, social and economic power
3 Enhanced political regionalization (EC and beyond)	Separation of political and economic interests; public funding of deliberative assemblies and electoral processes
4 Compulsory jurisdiction before the International Court; the creation of a new international Human Rights Court	Interconnected global legal system, embracing elements of criminal and civil law, with mechanisms of enforcement from the local to the global; establishment of an International Criminal Court
5 Establishment of a small but effective, accountable, international military force.	Permanent shift of a growing proportion of a nation-state's coercive capability to regional and global institutions with the ultimate aim of demilitarization and the transcendence of the war system.

If the history and practice of democracy has been centred until now on the idea of locality and place – the city-state, the community, the nation – is it likely that in the future it will be centred exclusively on the international or global domain, if it is to be centred anywhere at all? To draw this conclusion is to misunderstand the nature of contemporary globalization and the arguments being presented here. Globalization is, to borrow a phrase, 'a dialectical process'; local transformation is as much an element of globalization as the lateral extension of social relations across space and time.[18] New demands are unleashed for regional and local autonomy as groups find themselves buffeted by global forces and by inappropriate or ineffective political regimes. While these circumstances are clearly fraught with danger, and the risk of an intensification of a sectarian politics, they also portend a new possibility: the recovery of an intensive and participatory democracy at local levels as a complement to the deliberative assemblies of the wider global order. That is, they portend a political order of democratic associations, cities and nations as well as of regions and global networks.

New Forms and Levels of Governance

However cosmopolitan democracy is precisely envisaged, it is based upon the recognition that democracy within a particular community and democratic relations among communities are interlocked, absolutely inseparable, and that new organizational and binding mechanisms must be created if democracy is to survive and develop in the decades ahead. But there clearly is a danger, which the discussion of 'subsidiarity' in Europe highlights, that political authority and decision-making capacity will be 'sucked' upwards in any new cross-border democratic settlement. To avoid this, the principles governing appropriate levels of decision-making need to be clarified and kept firmly in mind.

The issues and policy questions which rightly belong to local or city levels are those which involve people in the direct determination of the conditions of their own association – the network of public questions and problems, from policing to playgrounds, which primarily affect them. The issues which rightly belong to national levels of governance are those in which people in delimited territories are significantly affected by collective problems and policy questions which stretch to, but no further than, their frontiers. By contrast, the issues which rightly belong to regional levels of governance are those which require transnational mediation because of the interconnectedness of national decisions and outcomes, and because nations in these circumstances often find themselves unable to achieve their objectives without transborder collaboration. Accordingly, decision-making and implementation belong to the regional level if, and only if, the common interest in self-determination can be achieved effectively only through regional governance. By extension, the issues which rightly belong to the global level are those involving levels of interconnectedness and interdependence which are unresolvable by local, national or regional authorities acting alone. Decision-making centres beyond national borders are properly located when 'lower' levels of decision-making cannot manage and discharge satisfactorily transnational and international policy questions.

Environmental problems provide an obvious illustration of the necessity of pursuing democratic governance at these different levels. For example, factories emitting various forms of toxic waste can be locally monitored and challenged, nationally regulated and supervised, regionally checked for cross-national standards and risks, and

globally evaluated in the light of their impact on the
health, welfare and economic opportunities of others.
Toxic waste disposal and global warming are examples of
two pressing issues which require local as well as global
responses if their consequences are to be contained and
regulated.[19] Democracy, thus, can only be adequately
entrenched if a division of powers and competences is
recognized across different levels of political interaction
and interconnectedness. Such an order must embrace
diverse and distinct domains of authority, linked both
vertically and horizontally, if it is to be a creator and
servant of democratic practice, wherever it is located.

Conclusion

By way of a conclusion, a number of points can be made
to help clarify the context of the arguments presented in
this chapter. In the first instance, the impetus to the
pursuit of an extension of democracy can be found in a
number of actual processes and forces, including (1) the
development of transnational grass-roots movements with
clear regional or global objectives such as the protection
of natural resources and the environment, and the allevia-
tion of disease, ill-health and poverty; (2) the elaboration
of new legal rights and duties affecting states and individuals in connection with the 'common heritage of human-
kind', the protection of the 'global commons', the defence
of human rights and the deployment of force; and (3) the
emergence and proliferation in the twentieth century of
international institutions to coordinate transnational
forces and problems, from the UN and its agencies to
regional political networks and organizations. Accordingly, it can be argued, a base exists upon which to build
a more systematic democratic future conceived in cosmopolitan terms.

To argue for a cosmopolitan future is not to claim, however, that it can be easily established. It has to be recognized that the meaning of some of the core concepts of the international system are subject to the deepest conflicts of interpretation. One consequence of this is the elevation, for example, in many international forums of non-Western views of rights, authority and legitimacy. Human rights discourse may indicate aspirations for the entrenchment of liberties and entitlements across the globe but it by no means reflects common agreement about rights questions, as illustrated in June 1993 at the UN World Conference on Human Rights in Vienna. In addition, globalization in the domains of communication and information, far from creating a sense of common human purpose, interest and value, has arguably served to reinforce the significance of identity and difference, further stimulating the 'nationalization' of politics.

But although there are serious obstacles to the realization of a cosmopolitan community, these should not be wholly overstated. In the first instance, scepticism and dissent about the value of ideas such as rights is often related to the experience of Western hegemony. Political and civil rights discourse is frequently rejected along with Western dominance, especially in those countries which have been deeply affected by the reach of empires. There are many understandable reasons for this. Understandable as they are, however, these reasons are insufficient to provide a well-justified critique: it is a mistake to throw out the language of self-determination and autonomy because of its contingent association with historical configurations of Western power.

More importantly, a cosmopolitan community, it needs to be emphasized, does not require political and cultural integration in the form of a consensus about a wide range of beliefs, values and norms. For part of the appeal of democracy lies in its refusal to accept in principle any conception of the political good other than that generated by people themselves. Democracy is the only grand or 'meta-narrative' which can legitimately frame and delimit the competing 'narratives' of the good. It is particularly important because it suggests a way of relating values to one another and of leaving the resolution of value conflicts open to participants in a political dialogue, subject only to certain provisions protecting the shape and form of the dialogue itself. Nevertheless, what clearly is required is a 'precommitment' to democracy, for without this there can be no sustained dialogue, and democracy cannot function as a decision-making process.

Finally, distinctive national, ethnic, cultural and social identities are part of the very basis of people's sense of being-in-the-world; they provide deeply rooted comfort and distinctive social locations for communities seeking a place 'at home' on this earth. But these identities are always only one possible identity, among others. They are historically and geographically contingent; for each individual, a different birthplace or social location could have produced a different national or cultural identity. Accordingly, for a plurality of identities to persist and to be sustained over time, each has to recognize the other as a legitimate presence with which some accommodation must be made; and each must be willing to give up exclusive claims upon the right, the good, the universal and the spatial.

The international community faces an uncertain future. It could be torn apart by the plurality of identities, public affairs becoming a quagmire of infighting among nations and groups wholly unable to settle pressing collective issues. Alternatively, steps could be taken towards the creation of a new international democratic culture and spirit based on new sets of regional and global rules and procedures – the constructive basis for a plurality of identities to flourish within a structure of mutual toleration and accountability. Certainly, there are many good reasons for being optimistic about this way forward, although there are also, of course, many good reasons for thinking that democracy will face another critical test.

NOTES

A version of this paper was previously published as a pamphlet by the Institute for Public Policy Research, London (October 1993).

1   See F. Fukuyama, *The End of History and the Last Man* (London: Hamish Hamilton, 1992), p. 200.
2   See N. Bobbio, *Which Socialism?* (Cambridge: Polity Press, 1987), p. 66, and R. Dahl, *Democracy and its Critics* (New Haven: Yale University Press, 1989), pp. 221 and 233.
3   See D. Held, *Models of Democracy* (Cambridge: Polity Press, 1987).
4   By a region I mean a cluster of nation-states in a geographical area which share a number of common concerns and which may cooperate with each other through limited membership organizations. Thus within Europe it is possible to identify the European Community with the political and economic boundaries of an emerging regional community of states and societies. While in South Asia, the Association of South East Asian Nations defines the boundaries of a developing regional complex.
5   D. Held (ed.), *Prospects for Democracy: North, South, East, West* (Cambridge: Polity Press, 1993), especially ch. 1.
6   C. Offe, *Disorganized Capitalism* (Cambridge: Polity Press, 1985), p. 286 ff.
7   A. Giddens, *The Consequences of Modernity* (Cambridge: Polity Press, 1991), p. 64.
8   Cf. R. Falk, 'The Interplay of Westphalian and Charter Conceptions of the International Legal Order', in R. Falk and C. Black (eds), *The Future of the International Legal Order*,

Vol. 1 (Princeton: Princeton University Press, 1969); Falk, *A Study of Future Worlds* (New York: Free Press, 1975); A. Cassese, 'Violence, War and the Rule of Law', in D. Held (ed.), *Political Theory Today* (Cambridge: Polity Press, 1991); and T. Baldwin, 'The Territorial State', in H. Gross and T. R. Harrison (eds), *Cambridge Essays in Jurisprudence* (Oxford: Clarendon Press, 1993).

9 A. Cassese, *International Law in a Divided World* (Oxford: Clarendon Press, 1986), p. 256.

10 C. Beitz, *Political Theory and International Relations* (Princeton: Princeton University Press, 1979), p. 25.

11 See Baldwin, note 8.

12 See Falk, *A Study of Future Worlds*, and Cassese, *International Law in a Divided World*, pp. 142–3, 200–1, 213–14 and 246–50.

13 One of the measures of weakness of the UN lies in its continuing dependence on finance provided by its members. The regular budget of the UN, excluding emergency costs, is some $8 billion a year. This sum is about what was spent on Western children last Christmas, or 'what US citizens spend a year on cut flowers and potted plants' (E. Childers, *In a Time Beyond Warnings* (London: CIIR, 1993), quoted in 'World in Need of a Transplant', *Guardian Weekly*, 6 June 1993, p. 10). The current cost of UN humanitarian relief operations and peace-keeping amounts to only about half this sum.

14 I have developed these arguments at much greater length in *Foundations of Democracy: The Principle of Autonomy and the Global Order* (Cambridge: Polity Press, forthcoming, 1995).

15 There is little chance of this happening, of course, while the suspicion is encouraged that the United States and UN are often interchangeable. Recent remarks by President Bill Clinton in this regard are singularly unfortunate. Reflecting on 'the lessons of Desert Storm', he affirmed that the United States would continue to play 'its unique role of leadership in the world . . . through multilateral means, such as the UN, which spread the costs and express the unified will of the international community.' Quoted in 'In the Name of the UN, Stop it', *The Guardian*, 14 June 1993, p. 18.

16 It is beyond the scope of this paper to set out my particular conception of rights, which I link to the notion of a 'common structure of action': the necessary conditions for people in principle to enjoy free and equal political participation. See D. Held, 'Democracy, the Nation-State and the Global System', in D. Held (ed.), *Political Theory Today*, pp. 227–35, and, particularly, Held, *Foundations of Democracy*.

17 See R. Johansen, 'Japan as a Military Power?', *Christian Century*, 5 May 1993, p. 477. Cf. Boutros Boutros-Ghali, *An Agenda for Peace* (New York: United Nations, 1992), especially pp. 24–7.

18 Giddens, *The Consequences of Modernity*, p. 64.

19 Three tests can be proposed to help filter policy issues to the different levels of governance: the tests of extensiveness, intensity and comparative efficiency. The test of extensiveness examines the range of peoples within and across borders who are significantly affected by a collective problem and policy question. The test of intensity assesses the degree to which the latter impinges on a group of people(s) and, therefore, the degree to which regional or global legislation or other types of intervention are justified. The third and final test – the test of comparative efficiency – is concerned to provide a means of examining whether any proposed regional or global initiative is necessary insofar as the objectives it seeks to meet cannot be realized in an adequate way by those operating at 'lower' levels of national or local decision-making. The criteria that can be used to pursue the latter test include the availability of alternative national legislative or administrative means, the cost of a proposed action, and the possible consequences of such action for the constituent parts of an area.

The tests of 'extensiveness' and 'intensity' follow naturally from the earlier discussion of globalization as involving both 'extensive' and 'intensive forms of interconnectedness. The specific formulations of the tests of 'intensity' and 'comparative efficiency' are themselves adapted from current European discussion of the preconditions which ought to be met in order to justify EC involvement in the policy-making process. See K. Neunreither, 'Subsidiarity as a Guiding Principle for European Community Activities', *Government and Opposition*, 28: 2 (1993), especially pp. 209–11, for a helpful discussion.

5
From the United Nations to Cosmopolitan Democracy

Daniele Archibugi

Introduction

Reform of the United Nations has been under discussion for decades. Although many reforms in the workings of the UN have been undertaken during the postwar period, really radical proposals, involving a substantial change in its functioning, have remained a dead letter.[1] The principal obstacle was the rivalry between the two superpowers, which paralysed any attempt to endow international organizations with increased powers. It is not surprising that one effect of the end of the Cold War has been a relaunching of the debate on the reform of international organizations, first and foremost of the UN.

The fervour with which reform proposals had been advanced after 1989 was quickly 'cooled' by the interventions under the auspices of the UN Security Council in some regional crises of the post-Cold War era, and most notably in the Persian Gulf and in Somalia. In other situations, such as the conflicts in ex-Yugoslavia and in some of the republics of the ex-Soviet Union, the UN has not taken any decisive part in preventing the outbreak of civil wars or in solving them. These cases do not substantially differ from the impotence experienced by the UN during the Cold War, with the notable difference that the lack of effective action cannot any longer be attributed to superpower rivalry.

Four years after the collapse of the Berlin Wall, the UN is far from playing the role of global governance for which it was created. Moreover, it has been shown that the law of the United Nations can lend itself to ambiguous interpretations. In some crucial cases, governments have misinterpreted it to support actions clearly at odds with those intended by its architects. It is not surprising that distrust has quickly emerged about the possibility of using the UN institution as a vehicle of international democracy.

Although some of the recent resolutions taken by the Security Council justify such a feeling, I believe that a central role should be given to the United Nations organization in the transition towards a new world order. It is neither realistic nor useful to imagine a more democratic global governance without assigning a principal role to the UN. There is no alternative to the UN as such, and its reform is needed to allow for better use of the organization.

This implies the development of two parallel and integrated actions: on the one hand, there is a problem of interpretation of the *existing* norms. The UN in its current form could already play a more relevant and progressive role in the management of international affairs – if national governments were willing to allow it. The legal principles of the UN Charter need to be restated to prevent a misuse of the organization. But, on the other hand, there is also a problem of reforming the UN to make it a more effective instrument of democratic world governance. Even with the most progressive interpretation of its constitution, the UN structure is not tailored to address successfully the challenges of the new world order.

Not surprisingly, recent proposals to strengthen the UN initiative have been made by a variety of sources, including the UN Secretary General himself.[2] The majority of these proposals, however, are more concerned with the powers of the UN than with its institutional design. This chapter is devoted to a critical account of the proposals made to reshape the constitutional structure of the UN. Their declared aim is that of eliminating, or at least reducing, those periodic oscillations in international relations which existing institutions have proven unable to contain. Even if they have little chance to be implemented in the short run, they represent an agenda for political action.

The reforms may be subdivided into three principal headings:

1   projects for giving voice to world citizens in international politics, and most notably for creating an Assembly of the Peoples of the United Nations, which would directly represent citizens rather than their governments;
2   proposals for strengthening world judicial powers, including the reform of the International Court of Justice;
3   proposals to modify world executive powers, principally the Security Council and the veto power of its permanent members.

These ambitious proposals have been widely supported on pragmatic grounds, while less attention has been given to the underlying theoretical rationale. This chapter, therefore, will concern itself more with the latter. The proposals to be considered belong to a specific current of peace thinking: that which proposes to enhance global security by creating appropriate international legal institutions. First, however, we need to specify both the potential and the limits of what I will call, following others, *legal pacifism*. Second, these proposals have a value inasmuch as they will bring us closer to a desirable form of world order that is able to satisfy the principles of democracy within and between states. We have labelled this agenda *cosmopolitan democracy*; its differences with the confederal and federal models of international relations will also be discussed.

Legal Pacifism: Underlying Rationale

A commitment to the value of peace unites individuals with various motivations, instruments and objectives. Full and precise taxonomies of peace thinking have been developed.[3] Legal pacifism, as one possible means for confronting the problem of war and peace, shares the merits and limitations of every judicial approach to social problems, being essentially normative. It differs from other forms of peace thinking in that it concerns itself not so much with the causes of conflicts as with ways of preventing and resolving them.

While social pacifism aims to pursue peace by removing the social or economic origins of conflicts, and religious pacifism by changing the nature of human beings, legal pacifism is an attempt to overcome conflicts by the establishment of specific institutions designed to solve controversies without violence. The use of force, if needed, is delegated to institutions entitled to apply laws. Legal pacifism has already been successfully implemented within democratic states, since they are founded upon the principles of non-violent solution of conflicts and enforcement by a legal state authority.

However, the judicial approach encounters special problems in the international sphere, which is a system characterized by the absence of a central authority capable of imposing a sentence on those – mainly states – who are found guilty by the court. Consequently, an essential part of the work of legal pacifism involves attempts to create supranational institutions with legislative, judicial and executive powers.[4] Not all advocates of legal pacifism, however, deem it necessary to create an international executive power. William Ladd, for example, held the creation of a legislative power and an autonomous international judicial power to be essential, but considered that executive power should be exercised solely by public opinion, which he optimistically baptized 'the queen of the world'.

From one point of view, the importance of legal pacifism is enchanced by the absence of an international executive power: while internal disputes within individual states may be resolved without recourse to force, since there exists an executive power with many instruments at its disposal to impose its will on the parties, in the international sphere there exist only two alternatives: either to submit to the decision of an arbitration which lacks the means for coercion or, instead, to accept that conflicts will be regulated according to considerations of political opportunism – not least the relative force at the disposal of the contenders.[5]

From this perspective of wilful worldly wisdom the merit of the judicial approach lies not so much in its intrinsic ability to overcome problems that result from inter-state rivalry as in the absence of more effective solutions. It is not surprising therefore that the battles waged by legal pacifists have been, at the same time, both huge successes and total failures.

The success of legal pacifism cannot be denied when we recall that today's international institutions themselves and the norms of international law are indeed its fruits. Institutions such as the UN and the European Community are much more highly developed than would have been imagined possible by those thinkers and philosophers who as early as the seventeenth and eighteenth centuries had envisaged international institutions with the responsibility for guaranteeing peace and cooperation between peoples.[6] The same goes for today's international law, which is certainly much more highly developed than could have been imagined from any seventeenth- or eighteenth-century treatise on the law of nations.[7]

On the other hand, the role of legal pacifism appears of scant import if we consider whether it has succeeded in holding in check and regulating international conflicts. For nearly half a century UN actions have been frequently ignored or circumvented by member states. In all conflicts, both great and small, both explicit and latent, the rules dictated by the *raison d'état* have taken precedence over legal principles. Indeed, the actions of the international institutions have proven effective only in those cases where an accord, implicit or explicit, already existed between the more powerful states. Where such agreement was lacking, the effects have been insignificant. In other words, the role of international organizations has been most significant when least needed, and irrelevant when most needed.

Legal pacifism has thus achieved an excellent logical construction, but one with little impact in reality. The discrepancy between precept and reality is barely counter-balanced by the fact that the former has become an integral part of international politics. The invasions of Afghanistan, of Granada, of Panama, etc., have been condemned by the international community and public opinion on the grounds of principles of law: without these principles, any condemnation would have remained exclusively moral.

Legal principles, in other words, are in part forced to be the precursors of reality by being declarations of good intent rather than of actual positive legal rights. These principles must therefore be assessed not on the grounds of their probable effective application in the world today, but on the grounds of their utility in an indeterminate future. Norms, even without enforcement, have their symbolic value.[8] The Universal Declaration of Human

Rights was a declaration of good intentions 45 years ago and still is to a great extent today but, by following its outlines, it has been possible on a daily basis to defend some fundamental and quite concrete principles.

Confederation, Federation, Cosmopolitan Democracy

Institutional design should not be interpreted as a device to face a particular situation. On the contrary, a commitment for institutional design implies that a long-term strategy is envisaged. While institutional design is often intended to be tailored to the interests of specific political movements or agents, I believe that this attitude is short-sighted and counterproductive: the actors of international politics change over time, and what might appear an appropriate institutional arrangement for a given balance of powers could be ineffective or even counterproductive for another. Once created, international institutions are unchangeable for a long time, and they continue to operate in periods dominated by different international regimes.[9] The United Nations, for example, was designed to promote cooperation among the victors of World War II, but suddenly had to operate in a framework of conflict rather than of cooperation among these nations. Nations can also dramatically change their role in international politics: in a few years, the Soviet Union has been led by figures as different as Brezhnev, Gorbachev and Yeltsin, and even the foreign policy of one of the oldest liberal democracies, the United States, has been inspired in less than 15 years by leaders as different as Carter, Reagan, Bush and Clinton.

International institutions should therefore be designed to withstand significant changes in political conditions. Although an exercise in constitutional design might appear sterile because of lack of support from the main actors in world politics, it will nevertheless help to provide precise targets for political action. In this context, I have assessed the reform proposals of the UN not on the basis of their feasibility, but in relation to what I consider to be a *desirable* global regime.

The perspective of cosmopolitan democracy requires us, in the first instance, to recognize the state as the central figure in international relations. The very notion of thinking and acting politically presupposes the individual's citizenship of a state; there can be no politics without a *polis*. Notwithstanding the fact that states may be imperfect institutions of human communities, since linguistic, religious, ethnic and cultural homogeneity may be lacking, they will always constitute the first and chief institutional point of reference for the individual.

The centrality of states as actors in international relations has not been modified by the crisis of nation-states that has occurred in the last few years. Although some multi-ethnic states, such as the Soviet Union and Yugoslavia, have recently collapsed, and regional conflicts which have emerged in countries as diverse as the United Kingdom, Italy and Spain are jeopardizing national unity, states still play a central role in international affairs.

The function of states is not only that of allowing individuals the right to participate in the running of the *polis*, but also, importantly, that of representing their own citizens at an international level. Individuals have no role in the international community, except as citizens of a state. As Martin Wight[10] noted, even the Pope, the individual who might be considered most inclined to set aside secular power, did not feel at ease in the sphere of international relations until he became the first citizen of a state. The tragedy experienced by the peoples of the former Yugoslavia and Soviet Union, as well as by those without states – the Kurds, the Palestinians, the Irish minority – makes it clear how problematic it is for individuals devoid of a state to have a voice on today's international arena and to have their individual and collective rights guaranteed.

Once it has been accepted that states play the role of an oligarchy in the realm of international politics, limits must be set. If the state, as an institution based on the inhabitants of a particular territory, acts in its own specific interests, then it cannot satisfy the needs of its own citizens if it is operating in an international community devoid of other institutions.

The first justification for the existence of the state is that of security: the *Leviathan* liberates the individual from the terrors of the natural state, and thus provides conditions sufficient for his or her acceptance of the role of subject. Following this observation by Thomas Hobbes, an organic theory of the power of the state has been constructed, positing the impossibility of extending the social contract beyond the state's frontiers and leaving international relations in a condition of anarchy.[11]

The weak point in the Hobbesian line of argument lies in the fact that individuals cannot be considered free from a condition of fear as long as they are still exposed to the threat of war: in other words, security internal to the state is not a sufficient condition unless a parallel security is guaranteed in relations among states. Until the state can eliminate the threat of war, its promise to liberate its subjects from the dangers of war cannot be considered fully realized, and consequently the subject has not the obligation of obedience.

In the nuclear age, the ability of *Leviathan* to 'wound' prospective aggressors can no longer be considered a method of fulfilling the above promise; as strategic studies have shown, the states least exposed to a nuclear threat are those who neither possess nor belong to alliances armed with nuclear weapons.[12] This is the crucial contradiction for the state: on the one hand, the full realization of *Leviathan* requires it to seal a pact of peace with other states, yet, on the other, the state cannot undertake this without significantly changing its sovereign power.

Still more problematical is the situation in those states which are obliged by their constitutions to fulfil the wishes of their own citizens, i.e., the democratic states. The absence of truly international institutions often presents them with dilemmas. Are they to defend their citizens' interests at the expense of other states, or are they to follow the rules of international democracy at the expense of their own citizens? They thus find themselves in a contradictory situation which can be solved only by entering into a contractual relationship with other states.[13]

To find a way out of such an 'anarchical society', political theory indicates essentially two ways of achieving an institutionalized system of states: the first is to set up a confederation of sovereign states, in which each member would renounce its autonomy insofar as its relations with other states are concerned, while the second would be to enlarge the experiment already undertaken inside the individual states, and thus substitute the multitude of sovereign states with a world-wide *Leviathan*.[14] Neither solution appears to resolve the unsettled problems of the international community.

The confederal model, which took global form first with the League of Nations, and later with the United Nations, is based on the principles of equal sovereignty of states and non-interference. Countries are represented by their governments, which are recognized on the basis of their *de facto* existence rather than on any grounds of legitimacy. Without these preconditions it would not have been possible to secure the membership of governments and countries with such widely differing political systems and values. The defects of this model are closely connected with its advantages: on the one hand, the principle of non-interference must be safeguarded to avoid 'the big fish eating the smaller' with interventions often dictated by pretexts; on the other hand, this principle sanctions the absolute autonomy of governments in their relations with their own subjects, and the total inseparability of the latter from the actions of their governments. Until a state breaks the rules of the international community, there exists no effective legal channel for censuring its activities.

It is not by chance that in the UN, itself blessed with a more advanced legal system, the traditional view of international law has prevailed, as was evident in the Gulf War: on the one hand, no sanctions for the internal abuse of power of the Iraqi government; on the other hand, sanctions inflicted on all the Iraqi population for a violation of international law committed by their government. In the confederal model, in fact, individuals are represented at the international level only by their national governments.

The failings of the confederal model are linked to more than the fact that some members have not been democratic. In fact, if they had been, the objective of the political struggle would not have been in the sphere of international relations, but rather the achievement of democracy *inside* individual states. The fundamental reason why the confederal model does not of itself secure international democracy is because each institutional state, however democratic, is forced to act on, and represent the interests of, its citizens on the basis of its own *raison d'état*.

Democratic regimes do not necessarily follow the same principles on the international stage: the United States and Israel have constitutions that are among the most democratic in the world, yet this has not impeded their violation of the most elementary norms of international law. Nor do dictatorial regimes necessarily behave in a like manner in their international relations: the former

Soviet Union, for example, carried out interventions not only in open violation of international law – as in Hungary, Czechoslovakia and Afghanistan – but also in support of national liberation movements, for example, the Palestinian cause and the anti-apartheid movement. In other words, there is not necessarily a concordance between a national constitution and international behaviour.[15]

The confederal model has traditionally been opposed to the federal state model. The extension of the federal model to a world scale is based on radical hypotheses, since it implicitly assumes that the existence of a constellation of states is merely a particular inheritance of history.[16] The elements which unify individuals across states are seen as important as those which link citizens as subjects of a specific state. For a system of states to be founded on democratic principles, its supporters affirm, it is necessary that there be the direct participation of individuals, for example, through the vote. The objections to this idea are twofold: the first concerns its feasibility, the second its desirability.

Federal states formed on the basis of a consensual accord of the parties – as in the case of Switzerland, the Netherlands, Germany and, above all, the United States – have come about from the necessity of concentrating their forces for defence against an external foe. However diverse their motivations may have been, these states figure as experiments similar to that of the Hobbesian *Leviathan*. Could therefore the same system function in a dimension devoid of external agents, such as the entire world? There are obvious reasons for doubting that the parties, i.e., the states, would be consensually disposed to transfer their forces to a central power – at least as long as states possess the attributes which characterize them in the modern age. It is of course possible for a federal state to be formed by the imperial imposition of one party on the others. However, if this state fails to conform to the rules of democracy at its inception, there is no reason to believe that it will do so once instituted.

As to the desirability of a world federal state, it is necessary to check how much it would be compatible with the effective operation of democracy. The concept of a state presupposes the existence of a unity of purpose in the norms applied by the several parties. For much of the world's population, these norms would seem alien to their particular historical and cultural traditions, and would be considered as authoritarian impositions. The creation of a world state, even in the remote future, can only imperfectly take into account the historical, cultural and, in the widest sense, anthropological peculiarities of the inhabitants of our planet.[17] The current crisis in multi-ethnic states probably constitutes the best indication of the difficulties inherent in administering large communities. Rousseau's empirical observation that democracy requires small communities in order to function should be constantly borne in mind.

Finally, the making of a world state with a monopoly on force, even if conceived and realized with the most perfect democratic constitutional engineering, would risk being transformed, as does any institution, into something at variance with the intentions of its founders. There could be the qualification, however, that this world state would have such a concentration of force as to render any successful rebellion impossible – but for this reason a world federal state becomes an aspiration which jeopardizes democracy.[18]

Could there be a third model, uniting the positive elements of both the confederal and federal models? Is it possible to limit the state's monopoly of decision-making at the international level without ending with a world state? The attainment of democracy at the international level requires us to steer between the Scylla of a mass of independent autonomous states and the Charybdis of a planetary *Leviathan*. Cosmopolitan democracy attempts to design such a model. It is based upon a new concept of sovereignty and of citizenship.

On the one hand, cosmopolitan democracy intends to put some constraints on governments' exercise of sovereignty. According to cosmopolitan democracy, the constrains on sovereignty should not be exercised by other states, as is currently occurring in international relations in spite of *de jure* sovereignty, but rather by legally authorized transnational organizations. In some areas of policy-making, this can effectively be done by intergovernmental action. Other and more ambitious issues require legitimization by the global civil society.

To achieve this goal, the inhabitants of the planet should be given a political representation beyond their borders and independently from their national governments. In order to do this, a theory of world citizenship's rights must be formulated.[19] Several of the events affecting everyday life of citizens are beyond the scope of their political participation because of the economic, social and cultural globalization of modern life. The specific route which leads to world citizenship suggests that the *cosmopolis* could be an end of history and not an attainable phenomenon – a political aspiration which must come to terms with the everyday actual citizenship, exercised by individuals within the narrower bounds of their own *polis*.

It is necessary to clarify that a theory of world citizenship is something completely different from a doctrine of natural rights. Any theory of natural rights is necessarily founded on a notion of the human being as outside a historical context and free of the baggage of social relationships to which the individual is constantly attached. Following the path traced by Rousseau and Kant, it is necessary to found a theory of the Rights of the Citizen, who at the same time is seen as a citizen of a state, with which he or she shares some historical and cultural values, and as an inhabitant of the whole planet.

The main aim of cosmopolitan democracy is to give voice to citizens in the world community in an institutional mode parallel to states. The development of institutional linkages between national civil societies would help to strengthen democratic procedures both in international society and within the single national components. But this does not imply that current states should be considered as a transitional form of political organization to be dissolved in a federal union which would have the same characteristics of national states but on a larger scale. On the contrary, several of the functions carried out by sovereign states should be integrated into the cosmopolitan model. On the basis of the model of cosmopolitan democracy, I will assess the proposals to reform the United Nations.

The Proposed Reforms of the UN

In the 1980s, only a few individuals and movements at the very fringes of international politics discussed the possibility of reforming the UN, while national governments and the diplomatic community hardly took into account their proposals. In a few years, the participants in this debate have drastically changed: national governments, international organizations and authoritative political institutions alike are currently discussing how and when the United Nations should be reformed. Conferences are held world-wide, and in some cases concrete actions have already been taken. Within this large body of proposals, I will pay special attention to those intentionally ahead of our time, and which have not necessarily gained support from national governments. Yet, they represent an attempt to create a world order based on consensus and legality, and they will constitute a fundamental component in the design of a democratic world order.

The following body of literature on the reform of the United Nations will be here reviewed:

1 the Campaign for a More Democratic United Nations (CAMDUN conferences): to date, three main conferences have taken place (13–15 October 1990; 17–19 September 1991; 25–7 September 1993);[20]
2 the conference organized by the Lelio Basso International Foundation for the Rights and the Liberation of the Peoples (Rome, 15–16 April 1991) on the theme of 'The UN between War and Peace'.[21] For more than twenty years, the Basso Foundation has also promoted an International Peoples' Tribunal as a method to deal with issues which were not effectively addressed, or not addressed at all, by official international judicial institutions;
3 the Stockholm Initiative on Global Security and Governance, whose conclusions have been published by the Swedish Prime Minister with the title *Common Responsibility in the 1990s*;
4 a study promoted by the Ford Foundation and the Dag Hammarskjöld Foundation on the institutional reforms needed in the ambit of the UN;[22]
5 the new UN Charter proposed by Harold Stassen,[23] one of the original authors of the 1945 Charter.

These activities promoted by civil society have recently been followed by a significant body of proposals and actions undertaken by official institutions. These include:

6 *An Agenda for Peace* by the UN Secretary-General Boutros Boutros-Ghali;
7 the International Tribunal for the prosecution of persons responsible for serious violations of international humanitarian law committed in the territory of the former Yugoslavia

since 1991, established by the Security Council with resolutions 808 and 827.
8 the institution of a Working Party of the UN General
   Assembly on 'the question of equitable representation on
   and increase in membership of the Security Council'.[24]

The following sections present a critical analysis of
reform proposals in the light of the most complex political
theory of legal pacifism. They will be treated in three
groups: those relating to the creation of an Assembly of
World Citizens; those concerned with the International
Court of Justice; and finally those concerned with the
Security Council.

A UN Peoples' Assembly and its Political Theory Implications

The most radical proposal from the CAMDUN conferences concerned the institution of a UN Second Assembly,
which, in accordance with the preamble of the UN Charter
('We, the Peoples of the United Nations'), would represent the peoples rather than their governments. This is
certainly not the first time that such an ambitious proposal
has been put forward: a World Parliament is an idea that
has been dear to philosophers for centuries.[25] In recent
years, however, a number of new proposals has been
made to the extent that a review of these proposals has
been found necessary.[26]

Most present-day proposals to create a World Citizens'
Assembly have been devoted on the possible procedures
for 'electing' this parliament rather than on the duties
with which it is to be entrusted. Indeed, paradoxically
even the subdivisions of electoral colleges are being discussed, but not much has been said about its scope,
powers and functions.

This is a considerable stumbling block since, as I have tried to stress above, there are robust theoretical arguments to justify and give credibility to such an ambitious institution. The forms which such a parliament could take are less important in comparison with its political significance, i.e., that national governments, who represent the states in the General Assembly, are not the sole institutions authorized to represent the citizens of the world.

The theoretical credentials of every reform project of existing international organizations, and especially those for the formation of an Assembly of the Peoples, are based on the recognition of the shortcomings of the confederal and federal models. These projects must be explicitly presented as attempts to give an institutional form to the model of cosmopolitan democracy, since they aim to allow world citizens to have voice in international affairs to complement the actions of their own governments.

There are also pragmatic reasons which prompt this institutional innovation. They may be summarized as follows:

(1) In the principal institution of the international community, the General Assembly of the UN, the electoral criterion of 'one state, one vote', is scarcely 'democratic': the vote of Luxembourg has the same weight as that of China, India or the United States. This means that governments which represent fewer than 10 per cent of the world's population, or less than 5 per cent of the world's gross product, may potentially cast the majority of votes in the General Assembly. As long as the General Assembly has little effective power (as has been the case up to now), one may easily put aside this problem by taking the point of view that the important decisions are taken by the Security Council – or, more realistically, by the superpowers. However, if we are to increase the real power of

the United Nations, the problem of the differing sizes of states must be confronted one way or another.

If it is assumed that governments should be the only institutions to represent their own citizens, the problem could be easily solved without creating a new institution, simply by giving weighted votes, according to population and/or other criteria, to the governments of each country in the General Assembly. For example, to strengthen the political role of the General Assembly, Stassen[27] has proposed the weighting of states' votes according to a composite index which includes population, national income and productivity growth.

However, the problem of the differing sizes of states needs to be tackled more radically, leaving aside a confederal logic; in other words, by creating a parallel body to serve as the expression of individuals and not of their governments. The making of such an institution will also allow the question of interference to be put in the right context. On the one hand, this institution will be allowed to interfere, with peaceful means, in the internal affairs of each state to protect human rights, minorities, etc. On the other hand, it will not allow single states to interfere, for their own interests, in the internal affairs of other sovereign states, enforcing one of the oldest norms of international law.

On a limited scale, an experiment of this type has already been realized within the European Community. This is based, firstly, on a body endowed with effective power, the Council of Ministers, with the 'one country, one vote' criterion; and, secondly, on a body with limited powers, the European Parliament, elected by universal suffrage, and with the number of members roughly in proportion to the populations of the member countries.

(2) Countries are represented in the UN General Assembly on the criterion of their *de facto* control rather than that

of their legitimacy; in other words, to gain a seat in the UN a political force must hold *de facto* control over a given territory, without necessarily representing all the citizens of that country. Some have proposed to establish that only those governments which represent their citizens democratically may be accredited to the UN. There have been judicial developments along these lines: the failure to recognize the government formed by the *coup d'état* in Haiti, the proposal to withdraw recognition of the *de facto* government of Burma and to accredit the duly elected one, etc.

However, to abolish entirely the principle of effective control in bodies such as the General Assembly and the Security Council risks being counterproductive because it could all too easily lead to a marked divergence between legal norms and reality. The consequences could be unpredictable: how many of the current governments have the credentials to be members of the UN on the basis of a rigorous application of its own Charter and of the Universal Declaration of Human Rights? How should one treat governments which are *de facto* but not *de jure*? Should they be ignored by the 'democratic' international community, or be considered as enemies to be fought? In this last case, how else but by means afforded by other states? This certainly does not mean that the Security Council and the General Assembly should always recognize the governments which exercise effective control even when it is gained unlawfully. But it is advisable that intergovernmental organizations recognize governments on the basis of the principle of effective control rather than of legality, unless there are transient situations or cases of extreme illegality.

A body representing citizens would have much greater flexibility: those countries which declined to nominate their own deputies according to democratic norms could be excluded, and in controversial cases the Assembly of the Peoples would have the authority to accredit the political forces deemed to be the proper representatives of the population. By means of its very existence the Assembly of Peoples would constitute an instrument of censure towards autocratic governments, who would see their own citizens voicing opposing views to those that they were putting forward in the General Assembly.

(3) However, the efficacy of an Assembly of Peoples would not be limited to countries with autocratic governments. Even in democratic states there may be significant differences between the opinions expressed by governments and those expressed by the representatives of individuals. In the first place, the Assembly of Peoples would allow direct representation of national minorities and of the opposition. In the second place, it is likely that within the same political force differing tendencies will develop, with the national representatives in the General Assembly being more inclined to sustain 'state-centred' policies, and the representatives of the Assembly of Peoples having a greater propensity towards 'global' policies. Take the case of the European Community: the European Parliament shows a greater propensity towards 'European' or 'global' solutions than does the Council of Ministers.

The most elaborate and realistic proposal for instituting an Assembly of Peoples, and one which has gained the widest support, was put forward in 1982 by Jeffrey Segall and the International Network for a UN Second Assembly (INFUSA). No fewer than 94 non-governmental organizations have already supported it, and INFUSA has actively promoted it with a view to getting the UN Secretariat to institute a commission to study the conditions under which this proposal might be made to work.[28]

Segall's proposal suggests that the 'Second Assembly'

should be an exclusively consultative body of the General Assembly. In this case it could be set up without having to modify the existing UN Charter; Article 22 states, in fact: 'The General Assembly may establish such subsidiary organs as it deems necessary for the performance of its functions.' This means it could be instituted by the General Assembly alone, without requiring the approval of the Security Council (where it might be blocked by the veto of a permanent member).

The electoral system would not differ substantially from that pertaining for the European Parliament: a number of deputies for every country roughly proportionate to its population, even if 'corrected' to safeguard the populations of the smallest countries. In one illustrative scheme of the proposal, out of a total assembly of 560 members, the most populous country (China) would have 31 seats, while countries with up to one million inhabitants would have one seat each.

The electoral criterion proposed by the INFUSA initiative is certainly not the only one. Many other electoral systems could be adopted which would safeguard minorities and allow the assembly to reflect, within certain limits, the real power of the various world regions. Some have hypothesized a weighting criterion which would take account of the income of the various countries, reasoning that this may be a suitable indicator of their relative international power and influence. However, a hypothesis of this type would violate a cardinal principle of democracy: decades ago, income ceased to be an electoral criterion within nations.

Other projects foresee transitional devices. In one of these it is suggested that the non-governmental organizations recognized by the UN might constitute a Consultative Assembly. Another method proposed for permitting the direct participation of citizens is that of making elective at least one of the five members who make up a national delegation at the General Assembly. It has further been proposed that a national delegation should include members nominated by the opposition as well as by the government.

International Judicial Power

Several proposals have been concerned with the making of a more effective international judicial power. It is significant, however, that the proponents of a World Citizens Assembly are seldom concerned with the reform of the judicial power, and vice versa. This difference in perception, and also of the evaluation of the priorities to be pursued, demonstrates the urgent need for reaching a systematic and integrated view on projects for reforming international organizations.

Not surprisingly, the main body of literature regards the principal judicial institution of the United Nations, the International Court of Justice. As far as the proposed modifications to the Court go, one can only remark that there appears to be nothing new under the sun, in that they do not diverge significantly from those already suggested by Hans Kelsen.[29] Kelsen allocated a central role to international jurisdiction in achieving the non-violent resolution of conflicts. He was convinced that an international judiciary would be the first step towards a political world order: 'Until it is possible to remove from the interested states the prerogative of resolving questions of law and transfer this permanently and universally to an impartial authority, all further steps along the road to world peace are to be excluded.' At the same time Kelsen held that the formation of an international judiciary would be the line of least resistance, and would not encounter the same objections that states might pose to an executive power or a world-wide legislature.

Kelsen recalled that 'long before Parliament became legislative bodies, Courts were instituted to apply the law to specific cases', and that 'we have good reason to hold that international law . . . will develop in the same way as the primitive law of communities from before the development of the state' (p. 58); in other words, that judicial power predates legislative power. However, Kelsen may have undervalued the crucial difference between the national and the international situation, which, to repeat, consists of the lack of executive power in the latter. In pre-state societies, in fact, the executive power was antecedent to the judicial power. This difference can only drastically reduce the role of international judicial power.

The UN Charter, adopted just after Kelsen's work, largely disavowed not only his predictions but also his hopes. It sanctioned the existence of a core of world governance in a much more marked manner than could have been hoped. On the other hand, the Court became crystallized in an antiquated role and was ill-adapted to incorporate the more innovative elements of that same UN Charter. The Court's Statute poses precise limits on its jurisdiction: in the first place, its jurisdiction is limited solely to cases in which the interested parties decide to apply to the Court in terms of 'a model which is much more arbitrational than judicial'.[30] In the second place, the Court's competence is limited to relations between states; it does not have jurisdiction over cases which concern relations between individuals and their respective states.

The Court thus reflects a state-centred view of international law, owing more to the League of Nations than to the United Nations. According to Richard Falk's terminology (see Chapter 6), it is at best a judicial organ for inter-state law rather than for the law of humanity. The modifications interpolated in international law have rendered the Court completely baroque, and unable to carry out to the slightest degree the ambitious role that jurists had proposed for it.

The need for a more progressive international judicial power has often been urged. The winners of World War II had already made a fundamental step forward by establishing the Tribunals of Nuremberg and Tokyo to judge individuals responsible for crimes against humanity. At that time, the accused defended themselves, arguing that their crimes were no different than those committed by their judges, apart from being those of the defeated. They also argued that such a tribunal was not legally competent to punish them individually because they acted on behalf of their governments. The promoters of the tribunal replied stressing that the principles of Nuremberg were much more important than the tribunal itself since they intended to open a new phase in the conception of individual responsibility.

For more than forty years, however, very little progress was made in order to develop and generalize the experience started at Nuremberg. Over these years, the Nuremberg principles have been defended by non-governmental organizations such as Amnesty International rather than by national governments. Civil society has also applied the judicial procedure (based on publicity, contradiction and defence) by establishing public opinion tribunals, such as the Russell Tribunal on the Vietnam war and the International People's Tribunal of the Basso Foundation.[31] Needless to say they do not pretend to have any power of enforcement.

After a considerable period of lethargy, the Security Council decided with Resolutions 808/22/2/1993 and 827/25/5/1993, to establish another International Tribunal for the prosecution of violations of international humanitarian law in ex-Yugoslavia. This tribunal has some analogies with as well as differences from the Nuremberg one:

1   it is *ad hoc*, i.e., it has a mandate for crimes committed in a
    limited region of the world and over a limited period of time;
2   it is not based upon a recognized positive humanitarian law;
3   the tribunal is not established by the winners of the conflict
    but by a third and more authoritative party such as the
    Security Council. Consequently, all parties involved in the
    conflict are potentially under judgement;
4   the accused are not at the bar. The Court is not in the
    position to have the sentence enforced, and it is unlikely
    that the convicted will be punished.

From a judicial viewpoint, it is easy to point out the
shortcomings of such a tribunal. It is not clear, for
example, why the Security Council has established a penal
tribunal for ex-Yugoslavia and not for another region. The
legal protection of human rights should in fact be based
upon the certainty of a jurisdiction all over the world, and
therefore should be protected by a permanent and mandatory tribunal.

The importance of the tribunal for ex-Yugoslavia, however, does not rely on its ability to punish a handful of
criminals but rather to constitute another precedent
towards the making of a cosmopolitan law. It will be very
disappointing if, after the occasion already lost with the
Nuremberg Tribunal, this second chance to create an
international penal tribunal is also lost. The experience of
the tribunal for ex-Yugoslavia should therefore be
generalized.

This necessarily implies a deep reform of the main
judicial organ of the United Nations, the International
Court of Justice. Three profound transformations are
required, which may be summarized as follows:

(1) Returning to Kelsen's suggestion, the Court's jurisdiction should be made mandatory. It is evident that passing
a verdict on matters between states is of little practical use

unless this is accompanied by measures against it (e.g., sanctions); but these would have a judicial (and thus a political) merit, above all in cases where the Security Council is unable to approve a resolution owing to the veto of one of its permanent members.

(2) The Court must furthermore extend its jurisdiction to cover cases which concern the relationship between individuals and their governments. It is absurd that, within the existing order of the UN, individuals must be safeguarded in their relations with their own governments by non-judicial bodies, such as, for example, the Commission on Human Rights. This means abandoning the human rights sanctioned by the Universal Declaration, and ratified by numerous conventions, to the exclusive sphere of inter-state relations, and thus to the inflexible laws of *raison d'état*.

Rendering the Court a competent judicial body obviously has broad theoretical significance. It would indicate that relations between a state and its citizens also concern the world community, up to the point that this possesses a judicial body independent of both states and inter-state organizations. The Court would thus be a body genuinely exercising cosmopolitan law.[32]

It may be objected that widening the competence of the Court to embrace individuals would lead to its becoming so overwhelmed with cases that it would be unable to function. However, once it has been accepted that individuals have the right to turn to supranational judicial bodies to safeguard themselves in respect of their governments, many expedients may be found to enable the Court to function. Ferrajoli and Senese have suggested that access might be granted to the Court to a selected number of designated non-governmental organizations such as Amnesty International and the Basso International Foundation. Another criterion might allow individuals to have recourse to the Court after national legal channels had been exhausted, following the procedures already in use at the European Court. A third criterion might be to consider cases collectively rather than individually, and to give hearings to groups of persons against their governments (for example, the Argentinian 'desaparecidos'; banned political organizations; racial, political and religious minorites, etc.). In short, these proposals are not intended to make this body some sort of Planetary Court of Appeal. Its function would be much more effective if it concentrated on flagrant and recurrent cases of the violation of human rights.

(3) Finally, it is necessary again to take up Kelsen's idea of governmental individual responsibility for war criminals and for war crimes.[33] Ferrajoli and Senese have proposed a significant extension of Kelsen's idea of enlarging individual responsibility in governments to all breaches of human rights. There are already significant cases where 'crusading judges' in some countries have, on the basis of radical interpretations of existing law, condemned those responsible for crimes against human rights in other countries.[34] These cases are significant because the criminals have been both condemned and sentenced in a country different from that in which the offence was committed. On the other hand, even though these cases may be important, since they appear to be a prelude to a new legal system, they are based on profoundly restrictive criteria and are unlikely to be substantially extended.

It is not by chance that the greater part of these 'crusading judges of international law' come from the more powerful countries, and especially the United States; the sentences they hand down place a great deal of faith in the existing balance of power between states. The judge of a stronger state may condemn the torturer of the weaker, but we can be sure that the reverse does not apply. Noriega is a case in point: there is certainly no shortage of good reasons for the Panamanian dictator to be tried by an international tribunal or even a US one, but there are at least equally good reasons for President Bush being tried before a Panamanian court. This supports the role of a permanent and universal Court independent from individual states.

Again, the Court would not have a possibility of directly applying a sentence: in other words, the Court would not have at its disposal the executive powers to imprison a guilty or aggressor dictator and his cohorts, but only the power to condemn him or her. However, even that condemnation would mark an important first step as a deterrent against committing crimes against human rights: following the condemnation, any legitimate authority could be authorized to implement it. Once the independence of the judicial authority had been established, then the function of the 'secular arm' could be delegated to the states in the absence of a world executive power.[35]

Introducing the principle of individual responsibility would mean establishing correspondence at the international level between the rights of the individual citizen and the duties of other citizens, at least as far as these represent the non-violation of the rights laid down in the Universal Declaration. In practice this would apply to that restricted group of citizens who are able to escape national justice because they themselves hold executive power: that is to say, those citizens who perform the function of governors.

Proposals for the Reform of the Security Council

The UN Security Council is, according to the existing Charter, the body with responsibility for taking executive decisions. Decisions on non-procedural questions are taken on a vote of nine out of 15, but must include a favourable vote by all the five permanent members. Aside from any judicial euphemisms, the permanent members hold the right to veto all the decisions of the Security Council. As a result of the existing procedures, permanent members avoid the embarrassment of declaring the decision of the majority invalid since only one contrary vote will fulfil this function.

The victors of World War II have arrogated to themselves crucial power over this body of their own creation.[36] Here we are confronted by something with no democratic justification: in no other constitution or organization founded on democratic principles is it accepted that a few members alone may invalidate the decisions of the majority. To understand the legal absurdity of this it is sufficient to imagine what would happen if the power of veto existed within a national political system: it is not easy to imagine a national government where the ministers of some regions could exercise veto power.

Not only this, but the way in which the superpowers have exercised the veto within the Security Council has far exceeded the intentions of the 1945 Charter. This laid down that: (1) decisions on procedural matters should be taken on a majority vote of nine out of 15, without requiring an affirmative vote by permanent members (Art. 27, par. 2); (2) parties to a dispute must abstain from voting (Art. 27, par. 3), as every legal logic dictates. In practice the permanent members arrogated to themselves the right of deciding both which matters were procedural and which were substantive, and whether or not to vote in cases where they were directly involved, thus blocking all resolutions against themselves.

The existence of the veto power also contravenes one of the supposed principles of the UN Charter, which stipulates the equal sovereignty of states (Art. 2, par. 1).

It is not therefore surprising that ever since 1945 both smaller states and jurists have been opposed to it. The prominent name is once again Hans Kelsen,[37] who, furthermore, has exercised a crucial role as an ideologue of the United Nations. Of course, it may be argued that a legalistic critique of the veto power is not relevant since it concerns relations which are political rather than strictly legalistic.

At the end of World War II the power of veto could be interpreted as a legal codification of the agreed status quo, with the victorious powers not wishing to oppose each other's freedom of action. If this legal abuse of power had succeeded in halting conflicts, it might have had some justification. It would certainly not have been better to have had a Security Council founded securely on democratic principles, but which had also helped to bring about a war between the superpowers: the motto *Fiat justitia, pereat mundus* constantly reminds us to temper the desirable with the practicable. However, even if we should judge the power of veto on grounds of its practicality rather than its rationality, it can be considered today only as a sterile inheritance of the past rather than as an element of international stability.

The world picture has changed profoundly since the end of World War II, and the decline of some powers has seen the rise of others. In the West, the most emblematic case has been the relative decline of the United Kingdom and France and the rise, above all economically, of Japan and Germany. Outside the Western world the role of developing countries has increased enormously in terms of population, wealth and military power. The UN had 51 member countries in 1945; in 1994 it has 184. The most significant change has occurred in the East, with the dissolution of the Soviet Union and of its alliance system. Apart from the entry of the People's Republic of China into the Security Council, no other change on the world scene has so affected the permanent members of the Security Council.

In this new international political situation, the present structure of the Security Council represents the principal obstacle to the smooth functioning of the UN. Today it is unacceptable to preserve the political balance of power resulting from the end of World War II, and we should wonder whether it is now time to make the abolition of the veto a principal political objective of the movement for a democratic world order.

Various proposals for modifying the Security Council have accumulated over the years, but they have remained a dead letter, given that every modification to the UN Charter requires a vote in favour by all the permanent members of the Security Council (Articles 108 and 109, par. 2). This being so, under the terms of the Charter, the General Assembly itself has no sovereign power over the UN constitution. In this situation, every proposal must take account of the power at the disposal of the permanent members.

For several years, the majority of these proposals were made by non-governmental organizations at the fringes of international politics, such as CAMDUN. Only recently the major powers have declared their willingness to accept changes. President Clinton, for example, has declared that the United States is favourable to giving Japan and Germany a permanent seat on the Security Council. With resolution 47/62, the General Assembly has instituted a Working Party on 'the question of equitable representation on and increase in membership of the Security Council'. Nearly one hundred written replies were submitted by member states, several of which echo the proposals made by the CAMDUN campaign. In a few years, the question of the composition and powers of the Security Council has become an integral part of the agenda of international diplomacy, up to the point that some states aim at 1995, the fiftieth anniversary of the UN, as a target date to implement the reform.

The general philosophy of these proposals is that the Security Council should to a certain extent reflect the world powers. Failing to do so, it is likely that major political decisions will be taken in other intergovernmental summits (such as G7 or NATO summits) which are much less democratic and accountable than the Security Council even in its current form. The tactical approach is to present the proposals in a spirit of compromise and mutual understanding, since it is clearly perceived that this is the only method which will allow them to be approved by the members with veto.

Let us now consider the proposals advanced both in the CAMDUN conferences and by member states, ranging from the 'maximalist' to the 'minimalist'. The latter may be legally less satisfying, but they at least have a greater chance of being accepted.

(1) The most radical is, obviously, that of abolishing the veto *sic et simpliciter*, leaving Security Council decisions subject to a qualified majority vote. Proposals to make the Council completely elective, thus denying the 'Five' not only their veto power but also the right to serve as permanent members, have received scant attention. Such a model would not only stop the Council from reflecting the existing international balance of power, but would also fail to enhance it democratically: we would imagine a Security Council dominated by the smallest states who had been notably advantaged by the 'one state, one vote' system in the General Assembly. Unavoidably, in a body such as the Security Council, which is entrusted with 'primary responsibility for the maintenance of international peace and security' (Article 24), there must be countries represented with the necessary force at their disposal.

(2) A subordinate proposal foresees limiting the power of veto of one single permanent member. It has been proposed that two negative votes of permanent members should be required to constitute a veto, or that in certain cases a veto could be overruled through specific procedures by the Assembly or by the unanimous vote of the other members.

(3) There is a unanimous consensus among member states that the Security Council should be enlarged. The prospective total number of seats ranges from 19 to 25. Some countries, such as Japan and Germany, have already manifested their will to become permanent members with veto power. But for the majority of countries the inclusion of two other countries from the North is unacceptable. India, Brazil and Nigeria are therefore participating in the race on the grounds of their size and of continental representation.

(4) A simple enlargement in the number of countries, however, will not increase the democratic nature of the Security Council. More progressive proposals have been made to go beyond the traditional state representation. It was suggested the Council should be opened to the existing regional organizations. A prime candidate for permanent membership would obviously be the European Community. The Security Council could include the existing regional organizations such as the Organization of American States, the European Community, the Organization of African States or the Arab League.

Some states have suggested introducing three categories of seats: permanent members, semi-permanent members based on geographical alternance (such as Brazil/ Argentina, India/Pakistan, etc.), and elective members on a regional basis. Others have suggested including new permanent members without the veto power.

(5) From the constitutional viewpoint, it was also suggested that the links between the International Court of

Justice and the Security Council should be strengthened in order to inform its resolutions on crucial issues such as threats to peace and global security. Some member countries have also suggested making the Security Council more accountable to the General Assembly.

(6) More radical proposals have suggested giving a seat in the Council to non-state institutions. It has been proposed that a World Citizens Assembly should be able to elect a member in the council, albeit with a consultative role only.

It is possible that, in spite of the declared good will of the permanent members, none of these proposals will be implemented, and that they will be blocked by cross-vetos. However, this does not diminish their merit. At least it will be clear which states are openly against the making of a democratic world order.

Final Considerations

This chapter has considered three concrete proposals concerning the United Nations: those relative to the formation in the heart of the UN of an Assembly of Peoples; those for reform of the International Court of Justice; and those on the modifications to be undertaken in the Security Council. The aim was to present an analysis of what legal pacifism offers to the theory and praxis of international relations.

These proposals inevitably lead in a wider sense to the efforts of those aiming to establish democracy in international society. Democracy at the global level does not seem attainable by simply putting together individual democratic states, nor by achieving a community of states without questioning their internal constitution. This justifies the proposal of an alternative model of international organization – cosmopolitan democracy – which differs considerably from both the confederal and the federal models.[38] Proceeding towards the realization of the cosmopolitan democracy model necessarily implies that states will have to allow, on a consensual basis, the world community to interfere in their internal affairs. In the long term, this process cannot but undermine the nature of the modern state, founded as it is on dominion over a given territory and population.

The perspective offered belongs to the tradition that, in a historical dimension, questions how to overcome the state as an institution. However, it also points out that the violent structure of nation-states is strictly related to an international society composed of rival states. The perspective offered by cosmopolitan democracy argues that the violent nature of the modern state, as well as its difficulty in fully realizing its promise of democracy, depends largely on its failure to integrate itself internationally with other states.[39] It suggests that a democratic state is an imperfect political entity as long as there exist no institutions able democratically to link its citizens to the citizens of other states. This is because a large share of the political problems on governments' agendas, including security and environment, are only partially addressable by intergovernmental organizations, since the interests of one part will often contradict those of the global community.

The debate on the proposals here considered is pervaded by two questions: can they be realized? And, if so, in what measure could they lead to a real transformation in international relations?

With respect to the first question, there is a good possibility that at least some of the proposals will, in the long term, come about. On the one hand, problems typical of our age – such as those concerning the environment and sources of energy, or those connected with growing economic integration – indicate that intergovernmental action needs to be strengthened by other less formal and more dynamic organizations. On the other hand, there is a perceptible tendency towards widening the international community, which implies an irreversible shift towards a progressive *de facto* reduction of the sovereignty of individual states. The significant shift in the attitude of international diplomacy which has already occurred in the last four years – from complete lack of interest to concrete actions to discuss some of these proposals – is encouraging.

History teaches us that the emergence of new institutions is possible only if there are specific interests working in that direction. The transformations occurring in international relations – the end of East–West bipolarity, the emergence of Third World countries as the subjects of international politics, the difficulties experienced by Western democracies in fully realizing themselves within the confines of their own state systems – lend weight to those political and social forces which have an interest in extending the influence and functions of supranational institutions. It is increasingly evident that decision-making is no longer the exclusive province of the *polis*. Any attempt to realize a model of political democracy within a single country must take account of the emergence of a global community: what the cosmopolitan democracy model proposes is, in the end, simply the creation of the appropriate institutions where citizens of the planet may discuss the problems and take the decisions that shape their destiny.

This does not necessarily mean that there must be a substantial transfer of power from the states to the new institutions. Not only would it be unrealistic to expect this, but it would not be desirable either. The challenge of the cosmopolitan democracy model is not that of substituting one power with another, but in reducing the role of power in the political process while increasing the influence of procedures. If we view the proposed reforms not as a panacea to cure the ills of world, but only as an additional way of confronting them, we may better understand their usefulness.

NOTES

I wish to thank Richard Falk, Luigi Ferrajoli, Niels Petter Gleditsch, David Held, Jeffrey Segall and Franco Voltaggio for their comments on previous drafts.

1 For a review of the 'realistic' proposals, see J. W. Müller (ed.), *The Reform of the United Nations* (New York: Oceania, 1992, 2 vols). More radical proposals were made, as early as in the 1960s, by G. Clark and L. Sohn, *World Peace through World Law* (Cambridge, MA: Harvard University Press, 1966), and by R. Falk and C. E. Black (eds), *The Future of the International Legal Order* (Princeton: Princeton University Press, 1969). For a comprehensive and critical overview of various generations of proposals, see R. Falk, S. Kim and S. Mendlovitz (eds), *The United Nations and a Just World Order* (Boulder, CO: Westview Press, 1991).

2 Boutros Boutros-Ghali, *An Agenda for Peace* (New York: United Nations, 1992).

3 Among them, I have found particularly instructive M. Scheler, 'The Idea of Peace and Pacifism', *Journal of the British Society for Phenomenology*, 7, 4 (1976), pp. 154–66; 8, 1 (1977), pp. 36–50; N. Bobbio, *Il problema della guerra e le vie della pace* (Bologna: Mulino, 1984); M. Ceadel, *Thinking about War and Peace* (London: Oxford University Press, 1987); V. Harle, 'Towards a Comparative Study of Peace Ideas: Goals, Approaches and Problems', *Journal of Peace Research*, 26, 4 (1989), pp. 317–51.

4 The separation of the executive, judicial and legislative powers in the international sphere dates back to such now-forgotten peace thinkers as K. A. J. Hochheim (pseudonym

Justus Sincerus Veridicus), *Von der europäischen Republik: Plan zu einem ewigen Frieden* (Altona, 1796) and W. Ladd, *An Essay on a Congress of Nations for the Adjustment of International Disputes without Resort to Arms* (London: Ward, 1840).

5 Bobbio, in this volume, Chapter 1, argues that the creation of a 'third party' in charge of arbitrating between two conflicting parties is already a fundamental step towards the making of an independent judicial power.

6 For an overview of these projects, see S. J. Hemleben, *Plans for World Peace through Six Centuries* (Chicago: University of Chicago Press, 1943); F. H. Hinsley, *Power and the Pursuit of Peace* (Cambridge: Cambridge University Press, 1963); D. Archibugi, 'Models of International Organization in Perpetual Peace Projects', *Review of International Studies*, 18, 5 (1992), pp. 295–317.

7 A comparative perspective is offered in H. Bull, B. Kingsbury and A. Roberts (eds), *Hugo Grotius and International Relations* (Oxford: Clarendon Press, 1990).

8 See F. V. Kratochwil, *Rules, Norms, and Decisions: On the Conditions of Practical and Legal Reasoning in International Relations and Domestic Affairs* (Cambridge: Cambridge University Press, 1989).

9 The most significant example is the Bank for International Settlements of Basel, founded in 1919 to manage German reparations for the winners of World War I and still existing today, in spite of the fact that German reparations have never been paid.

10 M. Wight, 'Why is There No International Theory?', in H. Butterfield and M. Wight (eds), *Diplomatic Investigations* (London: Allen & Unwin, 1966), pp. 66–107.

11 In the specific sense stressed by H. Bull, *The Anarchical Society* (London: Macmillan, 1977).

12 This point is stressed in G. Prins (ed.), *Defended to Death: A Study of the Nuclear Arms Race* (Harmondsworth: Penguin, 1983), and M. Kaldor, *The Imaginary War: Understanding the East–West Conflict* (Oxford: Blackwell, 1990).

13 This is a point emphasized by D. Held, 'Democracy, the Nation-State and the Global System', in D. Held (ed.),

Political Theory Today (Cambridge: Polity Press, 1991), pp. 197–235; 'Democracy: From City States to a Cosmopolitan Order', in D. Held (ed.), *Prospects for Democracy* (Cambridge: Polity, 1993), pp. 13–52, and in his essay in this volume (Chapter 4).

14 On the classical opposition between a confederation and a federal state, see C. J. Friedrich, *Trends of Federalism in Theory and Practice* (London: Pall Mall, 1968). For an excellent survey of both the theory and history of systems of states, see M. Forsyth, *Unions of States: The Theory and Practice of Confederation* (Leicester: Leicester University Press, 1981).

15 This leads to a number of ambiguities in the concept of international democracy: it may be understood as a *democratic* union of states, regardless of whether some or even all of them are autocratic inside, or as an *autocratic* union of democratic states. The concept of international democracy is discussed in the essays by Norberto Bobbio and Luigi Bonanate in this volume (Chapters 1 and 2).

16 See R. Hutchins, 'World Government Now', in R. A. Goldwin (ed.), *Readings in World Politics* (New York: Oxford University Press, 1970), pp. 517–30.

17 J. Thompson, *Justice and World Order* (London: Routledge, 1992).

18 Similar objections to a world government were already stressed by I. Kant, 'To Perpetual Peace: A Philosophical Project', in H. Reiss (ed.), *Kant's Political Writings* (Cambridge: Cambridge University Press, 1991). See also W. Berns, 'The Case Against World Government', in Goldwin, *Readings in World Politics*, pp. 531–44.

19 I have mentioned the Kantian roots of this attempt in 'Immanuel Kant and Cosmopolitan Right', forthcoming.

20 The proceedings of these conferences are reported in F. Barnaby (ed.), *Building a More Democratic United Nations* (London: Frank Cass, 1991); J. Segall and H. Lerner (eds), *Camdun-2: The United Nations and a New World Order for Peace and Justice* (London: CAMDUN, 1992); H. Köchler (ed.), *The United Nations and the New World Order* (Vienna: International Progress Organization, 1993).

21 L. Ferrajoli and Salvatore Senese, 'Prospettiva di riforma dell'ONU', *Democrazia e diritto*, 32, 1 (1992), pp. 243–57; R. Falk, 'The United Nations and the Gulf War', *Democrazia e diritto*, 32, 1 (1992), pp. 311–31.

22 B. Urquhart and E. Childers, *A World in Need of Leadership: Tomorrow's United Nations* (Uppsala: Dag Hammarskjöld Foundation, 1990); E. Childers, 'The Future of the United Nations: The Challenges of the 1990s', *Bulletin of Peace Proposals*, 21, 2 (1990), pp. 153–63.

23 H. Stassen, *The 1990 Draft Charter Suggested for a Better United Nations Organization* (New York: Glenview Foundation, 1990).

24 For a comprehensive overview of these as well as other proposals, see R. Falk, R. Johansen and S. Kim (eds), *The Constitutional Foundations of World Peace* (New York: SUNY, 1993), and Italian Society for International Organization, *Prospects for Reform of the United Nations System* (Padova: Cedam, 1993).

25 For a survey of arcane proposals, see E. Wynner and G. Lloyd, *Searchlight on Peace Plans* (New York: Dutton, 1949).

26 H. Newcombe, 'Proposals for a Peoples' Assembly at the United Nations', in Barnaby, *Building a More Democratic United Nations*, pp. 83–92; M. Nerfin, 'United Nations: Prince or Citizen?', in Falk et al., *The Constitutional Foundations of World Peace*, pp. 147–65.

27 H. Stassen, 'We the Peoples of the World', in Barnaby, *Building a More Democratic United Nations*, pp. 36–45.

28 J. Segall, 'Building World Democracy Through the UN', *Medicine and War*, 6 (1990), pp. 274–84; 'A UN Second Assembly', in Barnaby, *Building a More Democratic United Nations*, pp. 93–109.

29 H. Kelsen, *Peace Through Law* (Chapel Hill: University of North Carolina Press, 1944).

30 Ferrajoli and Senese, 'Prospettiva di riforma dell'ONU'.

31 The sentences of the Lelio Basso International Peoples' Tribunal from 1979 to 1991 are collected in G. Tognoni (ed.), *Tribunale Permanente dei Popoli: le sentenze* (Verona: Bertani, 1992).

32 In order to separate the functions of the Court as an inter-

state tribunal from its functions as a tribunal for human and people's rights, it could be divided into two separate sections, the first dealing with international law, and the second with cosmopolitan law. A similar model has already been successfully adopted at the European level.

33 Following the Nuremberg principles, the Statute of the International Tribunal for ex-Yugoslavia states that 'The fact that an accused person acted pursuant to an order of a Government or of a superior shall not relieve him of criminal responsibility, but may be considered in mitigation of punishment if the International Tribunal determines that justice so requires' (Article 7, par. 4).

34 Some significant cases are discussed in A. Cassese, *Violence and Law in the Modern Age* (Cambridge: Polity Press, 1988), and *Human Rights in a Changing World* (Cambridge: Polity Press, 1990).

35 Again, the Statute of Tribunal for the ex-Yugoslavia has incorporated this point. It is in fact stated that 'imprisonment shall be served in a state designated by the International Tribunal from a list of states which have indicated to the Security Council their willingness to accept convicted persons' (Art. 27).

36 H. Köchler, *The Voting Procedure in the United Nations Security Council* (Vienna: International Progress Organization, 1991).

37 H. Kelsen, 'Organization and Procedure of the Security Council of the United Nations', *Harvard Law Review*, 59, 6 (1946), pp. 1087–121.

38 D. Held, in 'Democracy: From City States to a Cosmopolitan Order', and in Chapter 4 in this volume, provides additional arguments for cosmopolitan democracy.

39 See M. Kaldor, *The Imaginary War*.

6

The World Order between Inter-State Law and the Law of Humanity: the Role of Civil Society Institutions

Richard Falk

1 Conceptualizing the Contemporary Failures of World Order

The notion of world order is situated between inter-state law and the law of humanity, although not necessarily at all in the middle. The inter-state is presumably the past, a time when clearly the inter-state dimension dominated our understanding of international law, but not the more distant past when states in the modern sense didn't exist. Perhaps, then, we should associate the period of the inter-state with 'the modern' and the law of humanity with 'the postmodern'.

The law of humanity is associated with the future; it is more a matter of potentiality than of history or experience. It is prefigured, and to some extent embodied, in the substance and theory of the international law of human rights. Its formal reality has been established through the primary agency of states and qualifies as a domain of inter-state law. But the historical potency of the international law of human rights is predominantly a consequence of its implementation through the agency of civil society.

This agency of civil society needs to be understood in two senses. Firstly, in the transnational non-governmental sense, typified by Amnesty International and the various regional watch groups – that is, voluntary associations of citizens using information about abusive behaviour on the part of states, exerting influence to obtain compliance, and, failing this, to disclose information about abuses that challenges the legitimacy of the accused state. Here, the preoccupation is with the well-being of the individual human being, and, as such, satisfies one aspect of the law of humanity (in contrast, inter-state law is preoccupied with the interests of the state as promoted by its official representatives).

There is a second dimension of the agency of civil society in relation to the law of humanity: it is the activation of peoples to pursue their emancipation from oppressive structures of governance, social movements legitimated by their aspirations being embodied in inter-state law. The movements of emancipation in Eastern Europe (as, for instance, Solidarity in Poland and Charter 77 in Czechoslovakia) were sustained, in part, by the realization that their most fundamental grievances had already been validated by the state that was offering such blatant resistance. In this kind of setting, the law of humanity is buried in the forms of inter-state law, but must be exhumed, and made operative, by the militancy of civil society.

World order, then, is a composite reality, reflecting the persisting influence of states on its normative order, yet also exhibiting the effects of voluntary associations and social movements that are motivated by the law of humanity and situated in civil society. The global spread of political democracy, with its roots in constitutional-ism, makes those persons within the territorial space controlled by the sovereign state increasingly aware of their political, moral and legal option to appeal to broader communities in the event of encroachment on their basic human rights.

The character of the law of humanity is not self-evident. It could mean law that is enacted by and for the peoples of the world, as distinct from the elites that act in law-making settings on behalf of states. Such a usage would correspond to 'the rights of peoples', the innovation associated with the efforts of the radical Italian parliamentarian Lelio Basso, leading to the establishment in the mid-1970s of the Permanent Peoples Tribunal with its site in Rome. Such an innovation is itself explicitly conceived to be a counter-institution intended to expose the abuses of states and the deficiencies of international institutions, and to provide civil society with its own autonomous voice. The formalization of this voice by way of legal instruments (for instance, The Algiers Declaration on the Rights of Peoples [1976]) and acts (for instance, the various decisions of the Permanent Peoples Tribunal) constitutes the substance of the law of humanity so conceived. In this regard, then, states are not regarded as appropriate agents for the development of the law of humanity, and it depends on civil society to establish new forms of law-creation and law-application.

It is also necessary to distinguish the law of humanity from the phenomenon of globalization, although there are some connections that will be noted as well. Inter-state law presupposed the autonomy of the territorial state, although such a presupposition was always a legal fiction given the hierarchical reality of geo-politics. During most of the period of the ascendancy of the state, the largest part of humanity was excluded from its protective structures associated for convenience sake with the Peace of Westphalia (1648), being subordinated within the frame of one or another variety of imperial geo-politics. That is, the inter-state system was primarily a regional system centred in Europe, and only because the region projected its power globally did the illusion arise of a world system. Ironically, it is only in recent decades, with the collapse of colonialism, that inter-state law became an encompassing global reality. The irony arises because, at this historical point of climax for inter-state law as a framework of formal membership, the realities of interdependence and integration undermine the presupposition of autonomy, rendering partially obsolete the claims of inter-state law.

There is a certain confusion that follows from distinguishing the law of humanity as 'the other' in relation to inter-state law. During the modern period the ideology of the state included the claim that such a system of distinct sovereignties upheld the well-being of humanity, that inter-state law was the best vehicle by which to achieve the objectives of the law of humanity. In this regard, inter-state law, with its positivist disposition, was seen as an improvement upon the naturalist approach that rested on a vague foundation of universalism that didn't correspond with the specific interests, cultural diversities and concrete values of separate people organized on the basis of distinct national identities. That is, the state reconciled the particular with the general in a satisfactory manner so long as territoriality approximated to economic, social, political and cultural reality. Of course, here too, adequacy depended on fiction as illustrated by the terminology of nation-state, a juristic conception of nationality that often obscured the presence within state boundaries of several ethnic groups with separate, often antagonistic, psycho-political conceptions of national identity. The state-fracturing impact of the right of self-determination when extended to 'peoples' (as in Article 1 of the Human Rights Covenants and in the post-1989 practice relating to the former Yugoslavia and Soviet Union) has exploded once and for all the misleading pretension of designating states as 'nation-states'.

But, arguably, the erosion of territoriality has under-

mined the major premise of inter-state law and its deriva-
tive claim to operate as the guardian of human well-being.
This erosion can be understood from different angles:
matters of vulnerability – the state has lost the capacity to
uphold security in light of nuclear weaponry and long-
range delivery systems; matters of environmental protection – the state cannot safeguard its territory from the
adverse effects of extra-terrestrial behaviour, nor can it by
its own efforts maintain the global commons (oceans,
atmosphere); matters of economic viability – the state,
even those that are well endowed and large, can no longer
provide an adequate framework for economic activity,
and is gradually being superseded by an array of international regimes and by the regionalization and globalization of capital markets and corporate and banking
organizations. In these three types of erosion, the well-
being of humanity requires law to be operative on a
regional, or global, scale that corresponds to the scope of
operations. It is here, however, that inter-state realities
persist, and the law of humanity is mainly in the dreaming
(or pure aspirational) phase. Inter-state law provides what
control there is in relation to war/peace and environmental
issues and, except for the European Community, with
respect to transnational economic activity. Thus, the
inability of inter-state law to rise to these challenges and
the failure of the law of humanity to take effective shape
is one way to express a critical view of world order; the
deep structural quality of these criticisms also helps
understand why even such a momentous historical
occasion as the ending of the Cold War and the reuniting
of Europe can have only a superficial relevance to an
enquiry into prospects for the emergence of the law of
humanity in an effective form.

    There is, in fact, a historically aggravating circumstance
associated with the end of the Cold War, the seeming
disappearance of strategic and ideological conflict, and

the focus upon world economic policy. Global security frameworks, based on inter-state activities, had been devoted mainly to the containment of strong states; inter-national law provided an underpinning, prohibiting recourse to aggression and validating collective security arrangements by way of either alliances or international institutions. There were many problems, including the difficulty of differentiating claims of self-defence from those of aggression and the unwillingness of dominant states to forego interventionary diplomacy, but the inter-state undertaking was coherent, and since World War II quite successful in the North, but it depended on the prevention of projections of military force across acknowl-edged international boundaries (the Gulf War). With the new situation of international relations there arises a preoccupation with the weak state, namely, the implosive realities of states that cannot maintain their own internal order in relation to either interventionary forces within their immediate region or secessionist tendencies of dis-tinct ethnic groups within their larger national population. The ordeal of Bosnia (or Somalia) is illustrative, with acute and prolonged human suffering arising from systematic criminality or from total breakdown of governmental capacity. Inter-state legal forms can validate 'humanitarian intervention' under either statist or international insti-tutional auspices, but the challenge of implementation can be overwhelming, especially in those cases where no sufficient strategic interest exists to provide the requisite political will to act effectively or where no geo-political consensus among leading states can be formed. In the process, despair and anger emerges, as we are aware of the inability and unwillingness to protect victims of abuse. Often only civil society initiatives are helpful in these settings, and then in ways that do not address the underlying conflict, as by providing humanitarian relief on a daily basis and seeking to identify and strengthen reconciling and democratically oriented social forces. The Helsinki Citizens Association has been playing an unheralded, but genuine, role in trying to build civil society coalitions that continue to seek alternatives to the violent polarization of Bosnian political space in terms of ethnic and religious enmity.

To some small extent environmentalism, as an expression of transnational civil society, has brought to bear the perspectives of humanity, encouraging and influencing states to establish regimes capable of protecting the global commons. Such transnational influence, as exerted by the Cousteau Society and Greenpeace and a coalition of other transnational associations, is responsible for safeguarding Antarctica from mining and developmental activities. The modality of the counter-conference, as evident at the Earth Summit held under UN auspices in Rio during June of 1992, has also been challenging inter-state complacency about environmental issues from the perspectives of the urgencies of humanity, but without any capacity to enact directly or indirectly appropriate protective law in relation to the dissemination of toxic substances, global warming or ozone depletion. Civil society performs a role as critic of inter-state law, but is incapable at this stage of providing a real alternative. Such limitations on the influence of civil society are even more apparent in relation to war/peace issues and to transnational economic activity. Note that the argument from a world order perspective operates on two levels: firstly, the eroding capacities of inter-state law to provide effective action; and secondly, the failure of a more responsive law of humanity to evolve, and the inability of transnational social forces expressive of civil society to fill the normative vacuum. I would depict the post-Cold War world order crisis by reference to this combination of circumstances.

2   Strengthening the Law of Humanity: an Urgent Challenge to an Emergent Global Civil Society

There are strong market-driven tendencies to constitute an effective system of global dimensions that operates to promote world trade and investment, and that protects the flows of strategic resources from South to North and that guards the North from threats mounted by the South. There are a number of policy arenas in which this phenomenon of globalization-from-above can be observed: the responses to threats against strategic oil reserves in the Middle East, the efforts to expand the GATT framework, the coercive implementation of the nuclear non-proliferation regime, the containment of South–North migration and refugee flows, the criminalization of 'terrorist' violence of a revolutionary character and discretionary status of counter-revolutionary terrorism, patterns of interventionary diplomacy that flow only North–South, the 'reforming' of the United Nations by concentrating authority in the Security Council and in the IMF/World Bank (while downgrading Southern priorities: eliminating the UN Centre on Transnational Corporations, marginalizing the General Assembly, UNCTAD, UNDP, UNESCO), the reliance on the G7 summits to set world economic policy despite the non-representation of 80 per cent of the world population. The law implications of globalization-from-above would tend to supplant inter-state law with a species of global law, but one at odds in most respects with 'the law of humanity'.

Transnational social forces provide the only vehicle for the promotion of the law of humanity, a normative focus that is animated by humane sustainable development for all peoples, North and South, and seeks to structure such commitments by way of humane geo-governance (that is, governance protective of the earth and its peoples that is democratically constituted, both in relation to participation and accountability, and that is responsive to the needs of the poorest 20 per cent and of those most vulnerable, e.g., indigenous peoples). To suggest the political dynamics associated with these conceptions, I propose the terminology of 'globalization-from-below' to identify these transnational democratic forces, and their implicit dedication to the creation of a global civil society that is an alternative scenario of the future to that of the global political economy being shaped by transnational market forces. The hopes of humanity depend, in my view, upon the capacities of globalization-from-below to challenge effectively the prevailing dominance of globalization-from-above in a series of key arenas that can be identified in very general terms as the UN (and other international institutions and regimes), the media, the orientation of states. Each of these arenas is complex, and needs to be deconstructed in several stages to identify the actual sites and stakes of political struggle. My argument in this essay is that law provides these agents of global civil society with one instrument of potential influence, and that the grounding of law so conceived is what is meant by 'the law of humanity'.

2.1   The law of humanity already contained in inter-state law, but not yet actualized

There exists in the corpus of inter-state law *latent* recognition of important ingredients of the law of humanity, making the latter function as a normative catalyst, and not necessarily as an innovative and idealistic alternative. This generally unappreciated potentiality of inter-state law can be illustrated by brief reference to four instances.

(1) Articles 25 and 28 of the Universal Declaration of Human Rights: there exists agreement among international law specialists that the Universal Declaration has been incorporated into positive international law, but many provisions are simply ignored, by human rights organizations as well as others. Article 25 confers the right upon every person to an adequate standard of living, while Article 28 confers an even more far-reaching right: 'Everyone is entitled to a social and international order in which the rights and freedoms set forth in this Declaration can be fully realized.' Even transnational democratic social forces that adhere to the mandate of global civil society have been silent about such *legally binding* promises by states. It seems desirable to break the silence, to speculate as to the shape of such 'a social and international order', and to insist that market forces be held accountable for upholding such standards within their sphere of operations and that states undertake to fulfil such legal expectations. That is, there already exists in inter-state law lip service to the basic ethical demands of the law of humanity (treating each person on earth as a sacred subject), making the implementation of inter-state law in this respect equivalent to the enactment of the law of humanity.

(2) Article VI of the Treaty on the Non-Proliferation of Nuclear Weapons: no international agreement has been given a higher priority in recent years than the NPT, especially by the geo-political leaders of the state system. Article VI commits existing nuclear weapons states 'to pursue negotiations in good faith' to terminate the nuclear arms race, to achieve nuclear disarmament, and, most dramatically of all, to conclude 'a treaty on general and complete disarmament under strict and effective international control'. It is obvious that this part of the non-proliferation bargain has been ignored by the nuclear

weapons states. Is it not time, especially with the end of bipolarity, for the countries of the South to insist on the implementation of Article VI as part of a reciprocal arrangement to forego nuclear weaponry that alone accords with international justice? Should not peace groups that participate in transnational activities organize a counter-conference to coincide with the 1995 NPT review conference to put forward the case for taking the legal claims of Article VI seriously?

(3) The Nuremberg Principles: the idea of holding leaders accountable for crimes of state was put into practice after World War II in the form of prosecutions of German and Japanese officials at Nuremberg and Tokyo; subsequent trials also held accountable all those in society who carried out the blatantly criminal policies of these states, including corporate officers and medical professionals. The Nuremberg Promise was to treat this experience as the first step in the development of an international law of personal responsibility that would bind all countries in the future, and not be applied only to a defeated power. This promise was given legal credibility by being adopted in the binding form of The Nuremberg Principles, first by General Assembly Resolution 95[1] in 1946, and then in 1950 by authoritative formulation by the International Law Commission. But given the belligerent practices of all of the victorious powers in World War II since 1945, it is reasonable to conclude that the Nuremberg Promise has been broken, although there have been recent moves under UN auspices to revive a Nuremberg process of some kind in relation to Saddam Hussein and to those in the former Yugoslavia associated with 'ethnic cleansing' and the systematic rape of Bosnian women. The forces of civil society have not been oblivious to the relevance of this Nuremberg experience. It was in the political consciousness of Daniel Ellsberg, who explains that a reading of the

Nuremberg Judgement convinced him of his personal obligation to release the Pentagon Papers during the latter stages of the Vietnam War, and, more recently, of Mordecai Vanunu, the Israeli nuclear engineer who released 'secret' information about Israel's nuclear weapons programme, was convicted in Israeli military courts of 'treason', and is currently being held in jail. Both Ellsberg and Vanunu have been acknowledged by global civil society in the form of awards of the 'alternative' Nobel Peace Prize, the Right Livelihood Award. There have also been a series of 'Nuremberg Actions', violations of domestic law to highlight criminal preparations by states for aggressive wars, as by the development and deployment of such allegedly first-strike nuclear weapons systems as the Trident Submarine and the D-5 warhead.

(4) The Preamble of the UN Charter, as well as the contents of Articles 1 and 2 of the Charter: the celebrated opening words of the Preamble 'to save succeeding generations from the scourge of war' represent a basic commitment to find other ways to resolve conflict than through reliance on warfare, yet UN practice, especially recently (as in the Gulf War and Somalia), discloses a disposition by states to endow the UN with a war-making role, to militarize the approach to security within the framework of the UN, and to downgrade, if not eliminate, the search for justice in the relations of states and respect for the dignity of each person in economic and social relationships. Here again unexploited normative opportunities exist for civil society initiatives, bringing to fruition the empty words of obligation accepted years ago by representatives of the leading states, and never repudiated or even questioned.

2.2 *Additional civil society initiatives needed to realize the law of humanity*

Realization of the law of humanity requires some independent visionary initiatives, especially to satisfy certain structural needs of world order given the scale and scope of international activities. This theme needs detailed discussion, and can only be introduced here in a preliminary fashion. An emphasis on geo-governance is beginning to be acknowledged in establishment circles that are primarily tied to the inter-state world: for instance, in the call of the Stockholm Initiative of 22 April 1991 for the constitutional renewal of the United Nations from the perspective of global governance; by the 1992 report of the UN Secretary-General, Boutros Boutros-Ghali, *An Agenda for Peace*, with its emphasis on a UN collective security process that is more independent of geo-politics than at present and on a strengthening of capabilities for preventive diplomacy that seem more feasible than efforts to resolve conflict after fundamental breakdowns in order have occurred; the proposal of Brian Urquhart to establish a UN Volunteer Force (outlined in the issue of the *New York Review of Books* for 10 June 1993, with further commentary in the issue of 15 July 1993) that could engage in peace-keeping operations (under the 'exclusive authority' of the Security Council and 'the day-to-day direction of the Secretary-General'), without present degrees of dependence on UN member states, especially the leading ones.

To promote the law of humanity, geo-governance must become a more organic part of the outlook for transnational social forces. There are two circles of emphasis, both associated with the interplay of functional or practical argumentation on behalf of global arrangements with normative argumentation on behalf of a humanely oriented sustainability.

There exists a strong distinct case for geo-governance as adapted to the specific realities of *environmental protection* and of *global market operations*. The prospects for voluntary adaptation of consumptive patterns and of technological choices in a manner that locates the primary financial burden in the North depends on having a much stronger institutional capability to set and implement environmental standards for the states and for the global market. Such a possibility could not even be put on the agenda of the 1992 Earth Summit, as states and market forces resisted such moves in the direction of environmental geo-governance. Only a concerted demonstration of commitment and need as part of the agenda of globalization-from-below could hope to fashion the inter-state political will to establish an equitable, yet effective form of environmental geo-governance. Legal specialists, serving the cause of the law of humanity, need to work out the institutional forms in helpful detail so that the process of negotiation can be encouraged on the basis of specific plans.

The regulation of the global market is even more difficult to achieve without the successful political mobilization and intervention by civil society forces. As matters now stand, the G7 states are committed to sustaining the regulatory vacuum on the global level. The abolition of the UN Centre on Transnational Corporations was expressive of this anti-regulatory disposition. Civil society is beginning to awaken to its responsibilities on these matters. The Permanent Peoples Tribunal at its Berlin session of 1988 investigated charges that IMF Structural Adjustment Programmes were encroaching on the rights of the peoples in the Third World, and the International Peoples' Tribunal to Judge G7 held in Tokyo just before the G7 summit of July 1993 issued a comprehensive indictment of the manner in which market forces currently operate, including the continuing practice of shielding money stolen from peoples by dictatorial leaders in secret over-

seas bank accounts and of allowing banks and corporations to choose tax and regulation havens in places such
as the Cayman Islands and the Bahamas. At present, civil
society forces need mainly to expose the abuses arising
from the regulatory vacuum and to resist globalizing
initiatives (NAFTA, GATT) that neglect the well-being of
the most vulnerable social sectors. The wider task of filling
the regulatory vacuum will be a crucial challenge to
champions of an emerging law of humanity.

The other set of structural needs involves the redesign
of international institutions, especially the United
Nations, so as to give greater weight to global civil society
perspectives. Again, this is too complex a matter to be
discussed here in appropriate detail. What is needed, to
put it briefly, is the weakening of geo-political and market
leverage on all phases of UN activities, with mechanisms
for greater participation both by countries in the South
and by transnational social forces committed to the promotion of human rights and democratization.

Reform of the Security Council has received attention
recently. There are statist and market pressures to give
the two financial superpowers, Germany and Japan, permanent seats in the Security Council, and some reluctant
willingness to give some populous states in the South –
India, Brazil and Nigeria are most often mentioned –
second-class permanent membership (presence, but without a veto) as part of a statist bargain. The orientation of
global civil society would go further, insisting on setting
aside a permanent seat for 'a moral superpower' (as
designated by a panel of Nobel Peace Prize winners),
another for a representative of the most economically
deprived states (as determined by reference to UNDP
indices), a third for a representative of global civil society
(as selected by a panel of alternative Nobel Peace Prize
winners), and a fourth to represent the world assembly of
indigenous peoples.

Other steps of structural reform are needed as well: reasserting the role of the General Assembly; establishing independent sources of UN revenue, possibly by imposing a transaction tax on international financial operations or on the taking of resources from the global commons; generalizing the commitment of states to accept the compulsory jurisdiction of the World Court and increasing the authority and binding effect of 'Advisory Opinions'. There are many more such initiatives that should be promoted by advocates of the law of humanity.

Efforts illustrative of more specific legally delimited initiatives are also important at this stage: the World Court Project that is being promoted by transnational groups to persuade the General Assembly to request an Advisory Opinion as to the status under international law of threats or uses of nuclear weaponry; a draft convention to monitor and eliminate the international arms trade that has been prepared by citizens' associations composed of lawyers and is being promoted transnationally.

3 A Concluding Note

Realizing the law of humanity is a complex, multifaceted, yet indispensable task. The main promotional energy will have to come from civil society, although one goal of transnational politics is to make states, mainstream political parties and global market forces more receptive to the claims and values being asserted by the advocates of the law of humanity. These advocates need to push their efforts strongly in two critical settings: the UN and the media. The UN is an ambiguous entity; its Charter can be read as substantially embodying the law of humanity, whereas much of the practice of the organization embodies the most regressive features of inter-state law, including deference to market forces, discretionary reliance on violence by geo-political actors and extreme selectivity and double standards in enforcement activity. Similarly, the media, especially in the atmosphere of democratic canons of legitimacy, is supposed to pursue truth without biasing its presentations for the sake of state or market, yet the reality of media operations (reinforced by patterns of ownership) is an acceptance of voluntary censorship to protect controversial statist undertakings from scrutiny and of refusal to delve deeply into most deformations wrought by the market in light of advertising revenues and managerial orientations of media executives. The UN and the global media are two sites of struggle or battlefields wherein the prospects of global civil society and the law of humanity are likely to be determined in the years ahead. The challenge is certainly formidable, but the opportunity is present to a historically unprecedented degree. Neither pessimism nor optimism can be validated given existing levels of knowledge, making the pursuit of the vision that corresponds to our values the most sensible course of action. And who is to say that its realization is less likely than the emancipation of Eastern Europe seemed a decade ago?!

Index